CONTEMPORAR

WITHDRAWN

CONTEMPORARY

Solitude

THE JOY ᴬᴺᴰ PAIN OF BEING ALONE

Joanne Wieland-Burston

NICOLAS-HAYS
YORK BEACH, MAINE

First published in 1996 by
Nicolas-Hays, Inc.
P. O. Box 612
York Beach, ME 03910-0612

Distributed to the trade by
Samuel Weiser, Inc.
P. O. Box 612
York Beach, ME 03910-0612

Library of Congress Cataloging-in-Publication Data

Wieland-Burston, Joanne.
    [Einsamkeit. English]
    Contemporary solitude : joy and pain / Joanne Wieland-Burston
       p. cm.
    Includes bibliographical references (p.   ) and index.
       (alk. paper)
    1. Loneliness. 2. Suffering. 3. Solitude. 4. Individuation
    (Psychology) 5. Psychotherapy. I. Title.
BF575.L7W5313   1996
155.9`2--dc20
                                         96-14631
                                            CIP

ISBN 0-89254-033-8
VG
Cover art is "L'Edition de Luxe," 1910, by Lilian Westcott Hale.
Oil on canvas (23 1/4 x 15 inches). Gift of Miss Mary C. Wheelwright,
Accession number 35.1487. From the Collection of the
Museum of Fine Arts, Boston. Used by permission.

Typeset in 10 point Sabon
Cover and text design by Kathryn Sky-Peck
Printed in the United States of America
02 01 00 99 98 97 96
10 9 8 7 6 5 4 3 2 1
The paper used in this publication meets the minimum requirements of the
American National Standard for Permanence of Paper for Printed Library
Materials Z39.48-1984.

TABLE OF CONTENTS

CHAPTER ONE
Solitude and Suffering, 1

༈

CHAPTER TWO
The Search for Solitude, 69

∾

CHAPTER THREE
Psychotherapy, 131

∾

INTRODUCTION

As I sit down to write this book, I am very impressed by the both vivid and varied experience in the domain of solitude that I know and hear of in the world around me. In my practice I see and hear daily how people suffer from solitude. This suffering ranges from a moment of desperation to a sinking feeling in the pit of the stomach which can hardly be described in its horrific dimensions. People feel absolutely alone, lonely, abandoned. Often the loneliness is triggered because the individual does not feel accepted or understood by family and friends. The fear of being left alone, of being abandoned by those one loves can also trigger generalized fears, and even be the major motivating factor of a person's daily life; this fear may determine even the minor details of the individual's existence.

I also meet people who speak of how much they rejoice in their moments of solitude, reveling in the heightened sensitivity they enjoy at such times, savoring the pleasure of being able to follow momentary impulses without the least regard for someone else's feelings or wishes. Still others yearn for solitude—some for brief excursions into solitude, oases to which they can retreat from the world for quick refreshment—others for more lengthy sequestration from a world which seems to them fraught with unpleasant social obligations. And, of course, I must also think here not only of patients, but also of friends and acquaintances who speak of their yearning to find a partner, someone with whom they can be; they very often quickly add that this beloved other should only be around from time to time: they need a lot of space. A certain well-measured amount of independence and, in consequence, of solitude, seems to be a desirable ingredient when mixed with just the right proportions of companionship. This appears to be a hallmark of people today: needing or expressing a need for close relationships combined with independence, for companionship and solitude.

I must think of myself here, too, and of the terrible suffering which solitude has caused at certain periods in my life, especially in times of separation and loss. The emotional turmoil which seemed to be triggered by real-life situations was such that my own interest in the subject was naturally spurned on. My joys in being alone at certain times, and for a certain amount of time, are less preponderant in my mind and would offer me personally less stimulus to reflect on the subject. But the fact of this paradoxical presence of two seemingly contrary emotional states connected with solitude—suffering and joy—is what fascinates me.

And now I know the joy of seeing how my baby, from his earliest moments on, seems to enjoy being with others, and yet also takes a certain pleasure in being alone. His reactions have known different phases of course, but he always seems to have liked to be alone: as a tiny infant he had the habit of lying quietly, sometimes not so quietly, alone in his bed, at times cooing, later singing, to himself. He would play with his hands, later with a toy. Pain at separation was first voiced later—around age 2—and although it sometimes sounded very serious, it never lasted for long. But perhaps these are my deepest wishes for this child just as much as they are my observations. I think it would be wonderful for a human being to be able to grow up to be an independent and yet also sociable person who can live and love him- or herself and others in company and alone.

As one readily sees from these descriptions of solitude that I have witnessed, there seem to be many different ways of seeing and reacting to this unavoidable human experience: it can be as debilitating as it can be enjoyable, and there are also many fine nuances in between. One might well ask here the often repeated and always difficult question: what is "normal"? Or, put in a less pathological framework of thinking (which I find more helpful for psychological inquiry in general), what can we call "typical" for the life of a human being? What is it about solitude that it can provoke emotional states that are so extreme and so varied? And why does one person suffer and the other rejoice in solitude? These are some of the questions which preoccupy me as I sit down to write.

People speak frequently and freely of the solitude of the aged. However, each phase of life actually knows its own specific solitude: infancy, childhood, adolescence and adulthood, as well as old age. And each biological phase of solitude, as I choose to call these succeeding stages of the experience during the course of a normal life span, can be painful and debilitating, exhilarating, and positive in its effects and in its feeling tone. In recent years, René Spitz did a great deal to make at least professional circles more aware of the depressing and even fatal effects that solitude can have on the lives of infants deprived of human warmth.[1] How adolescents react to solitude has often been a subject of concern, expressed by André Gide's *The Counterfeiters*[2] or today's widespread problems with drug addiction. Adolescents tend to experience solitude with a characteristic poignancy. Driven to desperation, and at certain times in history, even to epidemic proportions of suicide, generation after generation of adolescents and teenagers have reacted in their own extreme ways to feeling alone—seeking and reveling in it or fleeing it. They may choose alcohol, drugs, or acts of vandalism or suicide, depending on whatever happens to be the "in" thing to do in that particular period in history, to make a statement. One aspect of the ordeal (and I choose this word in awareness of the fact that it refers to a challenge often ritualized in pre-scientific cultures) is invariable—the intensity of their experience. That an important,

---

1. René Spitz, is a psychoanalyst, renowned for his studies based on direct infant observation. See *Genetic Field Theory & Ego Formation* (Madison, CT: International University Press, 1962; *No & Yes: On the Genesis of Human Communication* (Madison, CT: International University Press, 1966; René A. Spitz and W. Godfrey Cobliner, *First Year of Life: A Psychoanalytic Study of Normal & Deviant Development of Object Relations* (Madison, CT: International University Press, 1966).
2. André Gide, *The Counterfeiters* (New York: Vintage/Random House, 1973).

actually an essential, developmental aspect is involved is perhaps less immediately apparent: it has been well described by Fritz Riemann.[3]

Lovers suffer, young and old, from the absence of their beloved. Everyone who has ever been in love knows this. This kind of suffering has been praised as the proof of "true love." Poetic works, literature, and music repeat this idea over and over again. In our chronology of suffering, we move to the "empty nest" phenomenon which frequently coincides with the menopause; this basic and shaking experience of solitude leads women in midlife to confront essential questions about themselves, their lives, and their relationships. Men have similar experiences, but these are more likely prompted by separation from a spouse or disappointment in their career. The solitude of old people is legendary, for even in cultures in which the aged held a privileged place, older people tended to live a rather solitary life, being consulted by society only in times of duress. The natural withdrawal of the aged from the busy world led them to live on the outskirts of society. In our world today, the social exclusion of the aged is especially pronounced. In ghetto-like communities, old people wither away in a similar way to René Spitz's neglected infants—depression and untimely death often result.

As we see in this brief outline of the phases of solitude, not only suffering is involved here. The positive aspect of the experience can further personal development. Modern views of solitude often reveal common delusions, for it is a popular subject today. And, for reasons we shall be discussing in detail in chapter 1, it is on its way to becoming a subject of major concern for the world of the future. At least since the time of Kierkegaard, life has been seen as an epoch of existential solitude, per se. How can we understand the many voices proclaiming loudly the "charms of solitude," as William Cowper, in the 18th century, called the temptations of solitude? It is not difficult to acknowledge a deep and widespread sense of suffering that relates to involuntary solitude today; but we must at the same time note an equally intense and no less common striv-

---

3. Fritz Riemann, *Die schizoide Gesellschaft* (Munich: Christian Kaiser, 1975).

ing for solitude, or at least a certain quality of solitude. This quality is of the essence in the question: this solitude is to be well-proportioned, guaranteeing a certain degree of independence from others; of course, it is voluntary and not imposed by others. These differentiations make all of the difference in the world. If, for example, solitude is not voluntarily chosen, but rather is the result of rejection, then it is cause for immense suffering. If one feels too solitary—missing the kind of relationships one desires—suffering necessarily also ensues.

We live in a time when a pronounced emulation of individualism is leading many to take a stand for a voluntary type of solitude in preference to life within a community. The search for a satisfying, personally determined life style seems to be leading more and more people to choose to live alone. Concomitant is the widespread phenomenon of divorce. We are in the presence of a new sociological phenomenon: our society includes no longer attached or just plain unattached people and incomplete families, which constitutes a Singles' Society. Such a life style is common today; materially people can manage financially without having to live in a close-knit working community, but how do they feel psychologically? Furthermore, what are the deeper psychological motivations for this trend to individualism and more solitary life styles?

Psychotherapy bears witness to the difficulties which solitude actually poses for people. People seek psychotherapy, a form of treatment which intimately belongs to our image of the world today. It can actually be seen as a direct outgrowth of modern society's encounter with solitude. Freud's very first book on the subject of psychoanalysis, *The Interpretation of Dreams*,[4] marks the opening of the 20th century. "The talking cure," as psychoanalysis was originally called, definitely has to do with establishing a relationship with speech, self-expression; the accent is on relationship, in contradistinction to isolation, alienation, or solitude. Although solitude may not necessarily be the main subject of concern to the person who seeks psychotherapy, it is always an important aspect, if

4. Sigmund Freud, *The Interpretation of Dreams*, translated by A. A. Brill (New York: Modern Library/Random, 1978).

not to say the central, fundamental aspect of a basic problem. Solitude, and our reaction to it, is at the root of all psychological problems. Without a certain sense of solitude, nobody seeks psychotherapy. And so, it is of no surprise that the "cure" effected by therapy invariably has to do with establishing or re-establishing relationship, or, put in a more accentuated manner, with the retrieval of the individual from a position of isolation. This isolation is really more of an intrapsychic matter than an interpsychic one. That is, the sense of isolation stems from a divorce from one's own inner world; it is merely reflected in one's contacts with the outer world. But the former implies, involves, and actually causes the latter. Without being able to cultivate a deeper contact with oneself (C. G. Jung would have said that psychotherapy furthers the connection between the ego and the self, the center of consciousness and the center of the wider personality), one is unable to cultivate a deeper contact with others. Psychoanalysis reveals the tragic fate of modern people, torn between our relatively conscious search for individualism and our relatively unconscious yearning to be rescued from the suffering from our own existential solitude. In pursuing this widely acclaimed contemporary goal, people are often led into a position of extreme isolation. Sometimes a further step into a very much less desirable isolation is the unfortunate result at the far end of the scale. Oftentimes we find those who are actually unconsciously suffering from a deep inner solitude—in the sense of a serious divorce from their own inner world—speaking out in favor of such an extreme form of individualism. Their aspirations could then be understood as rationalizations of their own incapacity for feeling related to themselves and others, for forming meaningful attachments. But, being able to live out our own individual life in our own chosen way (in other words, living with a sense of individualism) has to do with being able to be alone and yet, at the same time, living in, or better yet, feeling connected or related to ourselves and to others. Nobody can really live a satisfying, individualistic life from a position of social or psychic solitude.

Another dimension to the problem of solitude has to do with the fact that any development, any creative process, requires a certain degree of solitude. No creative work—be it a work of art or a developmental step—has ever been born without a certain degree of solitude at some point in its elaboration. Solitude, or at least a certain proportion of solitude, is a necessary prerequisite for any development. Poets and artists need and seek a solitary retreat—in a studio, a garret, a landscape. The hermits and saints of old often sought spiritual transcendence through fleeing into the desert, to a mountain, or to cloisters, where they were closed off (the word "cloisters" stems from *claudere,* which means "closed off") from others. Even relatively "normal" people today, who are neither poets, artists, hermits, nor saints, need some silent place, some closed-off space in order to allow their creativity room for development. And this creativity can be as seemingly banal as finding our own personal solutions to problems of daily life.

Our attitude to solitude (as to all important domains of life) is extremely paradoxical. We need it; we suffer from it; we seek it; and we flee from it. Potentially positive, solitude is often painful, but perhaps it is actually the going through the pain which can ultimately make the experience positive and actually further the development of the personality. These paradoxes lead to important questions. How do we find our own, specific, individually measured portion of solitude—that quantity, and especially that quality, of solitude which we personally need in order to feel comfortable and satisfied in life? If solitude is really a necessity of development, how do we come to live it, or to live with it in a satisfying and fruitful way? And how do we find a relationship to ourselves that makes the unavoidable times of solitude, which are part and parcel of human existence, fruitful, or at least relatively bearable? These questions and others pertinent to the experience of solitude are the subject matter of this book.

In the first chapter we are concerned with the suffering that belongs to solitude. We want to discover just what it is that makes the experience so painful. We shall have a look here at various texts on the subject; on the one hand we want to show how people in an intact cultural setting can experience, meet, and deal with solitude. A comparison with our contemporary world imposes itself. Although the subject is far from new, it is essential in this context to describe exactly what makes our position so incomparably solitary, its demographic and psychological background (which naturally go hand in hand). From here we shall go on to analyze the component elements of solitude. An 18th-century poetical fantasy about a man stranded on a desert island, and a more recent biographical account of a prisoner in solitary confinement, reveal certain basic component parts of the experience of solitude. A fairy tale offers us a more dynamic (a more "process-oriented") perspective, for it shows the developmental possibilities inherent in solitude by illustrating the role that solitude can play in the growth process of the adolescent. Hansel and Gretel go through a painful adventure in the domain of solitude on their way to becoming realistic adults. In their story we also discover more about the psychological background for the pain of solitude, the unspoken opposite fantasies it harbors (in the form of symbiotic desires), and, therefore, the trap which it conceals. Meeting and learning to deal with the witch means becoming aware of this deeper psychological level of reality. Case material will help to make the application of the fairy tale and its implications clearer for us.

Solitude is intimately related to the question of self-esteem. Whether we feel rejected, i.e., exposed to an unwanted solitude, and, as a result, we feel completely worthless, or whether we choose solitude, withstand it and, hence, feel elated, even very superior, the truth is that whenever solitude is constellated, the question of self-esteem is always of the essence. In the second chapter, we want to research this other side of the question: the joys of solitude and the characteristic temptations inherent in it. A look at the tradition of religious retreat through the examples of Buddha, St. Anthony, and Jesus all point to common temptations in the choice of solitude, for (according to the Chassidic masters) solitude is the privilege of God alone. In choosing solitary paths, religious leaders are always emulating God, consciously placing themselves in a similarly solitary position in the hopes of being touched by Him, in order to reach the heights of transcendence. The search for solitude is invariably and in every context, religious or profane, part of a search for something higher, something greater, something beyond our present state of being. Fantasies of our own grandiosity are the temptation lurking there. A brief summary of the attitude to solitude in the history of the Western world shows that solitude has been cultivated as an attractive alternative to sociability throughout time. Our contemporary retreats are of the more profane sort, and are generally prompted by a search for individualism. On a less conscious level, they are probably often motivated by deep and repeated disappointments in relationships. The individualistic pose can reveal itself as a schizoid position with a strong mixture of unconscious symbiotic fantasies (à la Hansel and Gretel). In the same line we find a yearning for a symbiotic situation (especially in the form of a withdrawal after having been hurt by the world). Acceptable in this context is always the retreat to Nature, whereby we must realize that it is in the lap of Mother Nature that all "Back to Nature" movements have sought their maternal and symbiotic comfort after disappointments in the world of relationships (cf., the early examples Petrarch, Rousseau, and Thoreau).

Heroes are always solitary figures—from the early Greek heroes to the cowboys of recent lore, the supermen and private detectives of more modern fame, as well as the poets and artists living in "splendid isolation" in all ages. Heroes are not tempted by the world of merely human relationships. But maybe it is only people with difficulties in relating who become heroes. Cinderella is a dejected cindermaid with grandiose fantasies of herself. Although she does choose solitude instead of relationship at first, she comes to own up to her fantasies—to show that the shoe does fit her—and, therefore, becomes capable of a real relationship with the prince. Her developmental path is of interest for us here. Whatever the extremes may be, the fact is that solitude is also a necessary aspect of life, although few of us would dare say that we absolutely need eight hours of solitude a day in order to feel fit. But this may be so.

The third and final chapter is devoted to various aspects of solitude in psychotherapy. The first part tries to recoup the forced polarity of the first two chapters by pointing out the nuanced feeling reactions underlying the experience of solitude. I have tried to make it quite clear, but it must be stated unequivocally in this context: there is a great deal of ambivalence, or more clearly polyvalence, about solitude. But this is, in fact, a basic characteristic of human life, of the human being as a being of diversity. Generally speaking, people are not aware of the very diversity of the points of view dwelling within them: they do not often spontaneously perceive and/or sort out the various nuances of feeling dwelling within them. I speak here of two poles of the experience of solitude—positive and negative—from the point of view of the solitary. In reality there are infinitely varied mixtures of these two basic positions. But it seems to be part of the nature of humankind to have extraordinary difficulty in realizing the presence of other, less clearly outlined feeling reactions besides the mainly conscious one. When I think of my patients and what they say about their solitude, most either complain bitterly of feeling terribly alone or yearn to be on their own, for a while at least. Many "hold out" for a certain time in their normal daily setting, but "just have to get away," either for a week alone, or for a sabbatical journey to India, Nepal, or some other third world country with a strong spiritual context. Even the new generation of managers is feeling the need to "retreat," to indulge their need for being alone. Rare are those who are aware of the presence of other, less congruous feelings to solitude slumbering within. Few are those who can describe the bittersweet moment as such.

I shall go on from there to describe the goals of psychotherapy in terms of an image adopted from Virginia Woolf: "A Room of One's Own." This is the way Virginia Woolf described the kind of situation a woman needs in order to be able to write.[5] This is the kind of space in which creativity can be allowed to flourish: while the contact to ourselves is of major import, the contact with the surrounding world is maintained. To my mind, in psychotherapy we are seeking to discover the kind of space in which we can develop as individuals and yet not become closed off from the world at large.

Another image which I find helpful in the elaboration of a psychotherapeutic ideal stems from Donald W. Winnicott: he spoke of the necessity for the child to "be alone in the presence of anoth-

---

5. Virginia Woolf, *A Room of One's Own*, 1929 (New York & London: Granada, 1981).

er." Winnicott considered this the basic early childhood experience which enables a person to be alone. This silent and approving presence is a model for therapy and for the normal development of a sense of self. Case examples from my practice will show how typical problems with solitude (whether it be a deep and rather morose yearning for solitude, or a desperate suffering from feeling alone, panicky fears at the idea of being abandoned, or a fathomless and painful inner solitude) can develop and ultimately evolve within the therapeutic framework.

Every individual life contains multiple variations on the intertwining themes of solitude and relationship. The systolic and diastolic movements of these two opposite poles of human experience encompass the basic dynamics of our lives, from birth (when we enter our very first, primal relationship) until death (when we give up all relationships and enter our final, inexorable solitude). When our development is in some way impeded, we tend to retreat to a position of inner solitude: we lose contact with ourselves and with the world. Psychic processes then begin to unfold, which further contact with the inner world: dreams and other symptoms clamor for attention, trying to re-establish the interrupted communication, to start up the synergetic processes once again. In psychotherapy, we try to help people find their way back into the world of communication, of relationship, with the voices and aspects of themselves and with the outer world. Taking our own inner child by the hand, learning to listen to its sorrows and its joys, coming to care for it, is a powerful image that well describes the kind of attitude toward ourselves that favors development. It is an image whose central theme is relationship, and it is most likely based on the experiences of the child we have been with our early care-takers. One fact to which every school of psychotherapy can attest is that when this basic relationship to ourselves has been solidly established, either during early childhood or in a reparative psychotherapy, then solitude can regain its proper place at one end of the scale of human experience, alongside relationship. When this is not the case, and a basic, reliable relationship has not been established, then solitude can be a threat of indefinable dimensions to be feared and avoided at all costs.

The basic solitude of life in a civilization "without housing" (*Unbehaustheit*), as Martin Buber described our rationally oriented modern-day world, is a fact. In such a situation, the inner foundation of the individual—in the sense of the primary relationship described above—is of utmost importance. Again and again in the past the promise of solidarity in an illusionary symbiotic world has been a fateful temptation. Such promises have led masses of people believing in the fulfillment of these paradisical conditions to betray their humanity. The daily task of assuming our solitude is essentially a challenge to humanity. And speaking out with moral courage in our own modest and solitary way is a challenge which can only be responded to by people who have learned to be alone in the presence of another, to inhabit a room of their own. If solidarity within the human family can ever really be achieved, it is through each of us assuming our own personal, existential solitude.

CHAPTER ONE

Solitude and Suffering

THE NEED TO FEEL RELATED

*F*rom time immemorial people have suffered from feeling lonely and alone, from feeling abandoned and unloved. It seems that this must be so, and will continue to be so, for solitude is the other side of another typically human characteristic—the tendency to form attachments. We are born with a predisposition: we want to form attachments. When these attachments are lacking (whether they are broken off or just missing), we suffer. One can say, in Jungian terminology, that we are born with an archetypal need to form relationships or that the inborn human tendency needs to feel related—not only to people but also to things. From the earliest cavemen to the inhabitants of the most modern metropolis, men and women of all cultures know this need. When it is not fulfilled, we suffer from feeling lonely and alone—from solitude.

Some people seem to enjoy solitude, some even seek it; everyone needs to be alone sometimes. Certain people are able to be alone for prolonged periods of time without feeling utterly lonely and abandoned. Such a capacity is said to be grounded on a specific type of early experience which I shall describe in detail in the final chapter of this book. For the sake of clarity, I must mention, if only briefly, the fact that even if people enjoy solitude—preferring to live on the outskirts of society, in isolation from others, or merely temporarily seeking retreat—even then, they still very much need to feel related. The need can also be satisfied by relationships to things and beings other than human—to animals or objects,

4 ~ JOANNE WIELAND-BURSTON

books, paintings, music, culture in general, or even to personal belongings, like furniture. Feeling related, attached, connected to a certain physical space, a place, a type of scenery can also make people feel related to surroundings and to themselves.

The crippling effects of being denied the fulfillment of these needs are readily seen, for example, in refugees, people uprooted from their customary surroundings, who have neither family nor friends, nor even objects around them that feel familiar, and which they, therefore, cherish and feel "at home" with. It is interesting to note the ubiquitous use of imprisonment and various forms of more or less solitary confinement as a means by which societies punish their outlaws. That people suffer from such a form of punishment is obvious. Erich Fromm speaks quite unequivocally of the severe consequences of solitude on the individual. He says:

> To feel completely alone and isolated leads to mental disintegration just as physical starvation leads to death.[1]

That solitude can be as detrimental to the mind and soul as starvation is to the body is a statement of major import. We all know the distress of mourning, the pain of separation from loved ones; we all have seen, or at least heard of, the suffering of families who have been torn apart, of the depressive agitation or apathy of those secluded by illness or old age. Suffering from solitude is characteristic of being human. The complete absence of any of this suffering is more questionable than its presence. (Those rare human beings whom we find declaring their exclusive and compelling need to be alone are inevitably motivated by deep-seated mistrust, triggered by disappointments in relationships. Their suffering from solitude, quite unconscious, is compensated for by a sense of their grandiose position of "splendid isolation.") In quite general terms, we can say that for human beings, whether they are naturally very sociable or very withdrawn, when the need for feeling related is not satisfied, the person suffers from feeling alone and lonely; solitude causes pain.

---

1. Erich Fromm, *Escape from Freedom* (New York: Holt, Reinhart and Winston, 1941; New York: Avon, 1976), p. 15.

In this chapter we want to delve into the negative side of the experience of solitude. A look at earlier cultures will show us how solitude was met—experienced, expressed, and dealt with—in socially intact societies of earlier times. The comparison with our contemporary world reveals the influence that society and culture can have on perception and the experience of solitude. From there we shall go on to a deeper level of investigation, examining the component elements which go into making up the pain involved in solitude. What is so distressing about solitude? What are we really missing when we feel alone? And why does this lack hurt so much? Is such suffering "normal"? Can it be assuaged? Might there also be positive aspects to it? A 20th century novel and an 18th century poem will serve as the basis for this detailed analysis of the problem. From there we shall go on to look at a fairy tale, for in such anonymous popular creations we often find the elaboration of developmental possibilities for typical human problems. The story of Hansel and Gretel shows the dynamics of solitude as an inner psychic state: how it can arise, where it can lead, and how it can be resolved. In this context solitude, and even suffering from it, can be seen as an important, albeit painful aspect of the maturation process. This example leads us directly to the field of psychotherapy and to real-life examples; we shall look at some cases of negative experiences of solitude, showing the sources of the problems and the development made possible through psychotherapy.

Death in Earlier Cultures

∽·

Two basic life experiences have led people to suffer from solitude from the earliest times to the present day—death and exile. Both of these experiences have been, and will continue to be, facts of life. Both make us realize the extent to which we cherish and *need* a sense of feeling related in order to feel at home in ourselves and, hence, in the world. In order to understand this better we shall be looking in detail at three different texts. Two are very early testimonials to the way people have suffered, and how they expressed and tried to deal with their suffering. The comparison with our modern situation helps explain why solitude is often felt to be so threatening for people today. The third text is modern and shows more of what the lack of solitude can mean to us; in other words, what we are actually missing when we say that we feel alone.

The loss of a loved one is always difficult, whether this loss is provoked by death or by less definitive separations. Whether one is abandoned in a love affair, or faced with children leaving home, separation inevitably confronts us with painful moments of solitude. I would like to concentrate in this context on the suffering caused by the death of a loved one. One of the earliest extant texts in our culture provides invaluable insights on what this unavoidable human confrontation with solitude could look like in very ancient times.

Suffering from solitude was poignant and anything but muted. It was acted out rather than described in words as an inner state. Such powerful expression implies an audience, and it is precisely this audience which holds and comforts the mourner. It constitutes a social and spiritual community in the here and now, guaranteeing a sense of echo and understanding, and, therefore, actually precluding any absolute experience of solitude that people today might know. A feeling of belonging to a universe which is by definition also a spiritual universe echoes back one's own suffering and, thus, confirms it, makes it feel confirmed, accepted, and approved. This empathic presence of a caring world helps the solitary sufferer re-establish the connection to self and life which is temporarily destroyed by the loss of a loved one.

We could well refer here to Job whose suffering at the loss of family, friends, and property is well known and still moving today. Tearing his hair out, and strewing his head with ashes is Job's way of expressing his suffering. But the text of the Book of Job probably dates from the sixth century Before the Judaeo-Christian Era [henceforth referred to as B.J.C.E.]. Let us look at a less well known, but much earlier text. A large portion of the *Gilgamesh Epic* describes the reactions of Gilgamesh to the death of his friend Enkidu. As the model for Gilgamesh is thought to have lived in the land of Uru (southern Babylon) around 2750 to 2600 B.J.C.E., scholars reckon that the epic, itself, must have been written about 1700 B.J.C.E. The text is really very primitive.

Gilgamesh's reactions to Enkidu's death are recounted in three different phases. In the first place, Gilgamesh calls upon the community of people and things which surround him, which make up his world. This predominant position is significant in itself, for it shows that the reaction is spontaneous, first and foremost in the mind of the author, if not in that of Gilgamesh. These people and things are partners in an imagined dialogue, mute but nonetheless empathic witnesses to the hero's suffering. He calls upon them all, addressing them one by one and by name, pleading with them to help him mourn for Enkidu. "The cedar forest, the ancients of Uruk-Gart, the entire population, the men of the mountains, the floors of the forest, the forest itself, the cypresses and the cedars, the bear and the hyena, the tiger and the holy river Ulai, the pure Euphrates, the shepherds and the prostitutes,"[2] these are the words in which Gilgamesh appeals to them, asking them to help him cry for Enkidu.

This animated universe—a world of nature, of men and women, imagined as being capable and willing to empathize with the sufferer—bears evidence to the fact that though Gilgamesh may feel abandoned because of the loss of his friend, he cannot actually feel entirely alone. A community surrounds him; it can hear his grief and even help him express and, therefore, bear it. This fact of life is referred to directly in a phrase which calls up images which are perhaps more familiar to us. Gilgamesh says: "I cry for Enkidu my friend, like a wailing woman (*Klagerweib*), I cry bitterly." We know this custom of the wailing women from Greek tragedy as well as from modern films of Greece: women are hired

---

2. *Epic of Gilgamesh*, edited by Nancy Sanders (London: Penguin, 1960), pp. 71-72.

to cry at burials. This is one way in which the community can help mourn for the dead.

Gilgamesh also acts out his desperation. He tears off his fine clothes, throwing them away "as if they were something untouchable." Afterward, his grief overcomes him. Acting out is a physical and concrete way of expressing a problem. Speaking about it— articulating it—is a more psychologically differentiated, we would say less "primitive," that is, less crude and unsophisticated way of expressing one's feelings; developmentally speaking, verbal expression requires a higher level of consciousness and of maturity. Nevertheless, we all know that expressing rage by throwing something, "primitive" though the reaction may be, can be extremely satisfying. The fact that an audience is an implicit fantasy of acting out is a point of extreme interest in the context of our investigation into solitude. "Primitive man" (i.e., people in earlier or pre-scientific cultures) could count on the presence of an audience to witness their suffering, and this empathic witnessing of desperate feelings and actions confirms and approves them, giving them weight and validity. Generally speaking, modern people cannot count on such a presence. However, all group therapy, be it the Alcoholics Anonymous encounter groups, recovery groups, or spiritual healing groups, all rely on and profit from the special type of energy generated by the group for just this reason: confirmation, echoing, bestowing weight, validity, and importance on that which is acted out in the presence of empathic others. It is significant to note, and I shall be coming back to this point in a moment, that acting out is allowed a certain space in some religious rituals to this day.

In the second phase of his suffering, Gilgamesh appeals to another sphere of his universe: the more obviously spiritual. He sees some lions and this otherwise heroic figure suddenly fears for his life. He appeals to his gods and goddesses—Sin, the god of the moon, and to "the greatest of the goddesses" (as the epic puts it)— to protect him. Immediately afterward he has a dream: he sees a warrior and takes this as a message from the gods. He decides to set off, as a warrior himself, seeking the meaning of life and death. Questioning the meaning of life is a common reaction when a loved one dies. Here we see how his belief in the spiritual domain helps Gilgamesh believe that an answer can be found, that protection and communication can come from the gods. Gilgamesh is not alone and lost in an uncaring universe; the pain of the moment can be assuaged, because in his mind answers can be found and divinities can provide answers.

The third phase of Gilgamesh's suffering is recounted in the context of his spiritual journey. He meets various beings on the way to seek out those who have the answers to his questions about life and death. They all ask him why he looks the way he does. Enkidu's death has taken such a toll on him that he is even marked physically by it. In repeated mirror passages, we learn that Gilgamesh's cheeks are sunken; he is bent over, his heart seems sad, his tongue dead; grief is in his soul. Physical descriptions and figurative descriptions all reflect the state of Gilgamesh's soul. And his responses to the questions posed again and again by those whom he meets reveal more about his initial reactions to Enkidu's death. He cried day and night and did not allow Enkidu to be buried for six days and seven nights. And he adds that since Enkidu's death he has not found life, but has been wandering through the steppes "like a thief," seeking life. Gilgamesh's suffering is not unlike that of people today who lose a loved one. They, too, cry, refuse to acknowledge the death, find life no longer worth living, and wonder about the meaning of all of this. But Gilgamesh's world does offer some solace for the lonely sufferer.

However painful the loss, however solitary and abandoned a person in this type of culture felt, Gilgamesh's solitude can in no way be compared to that of modern men and women who, at the loss of a loved one, can really feel and actually be *absolutely* alone. Martin Buber would call this fact of ancient life the *Behaustheit*[3] of earlier cultures. In our context we can speak of the unsolitary solitude, or the *accompanied solitude*, of more primitive periods in history. On the one hand, the social community and even the natural landscape, animated and empathic as they are, can join the mourn-

3. *Behaustheit* means feeling at home in the world; living in the world as though it is a house. Martin Buber: *Between Man & Man* (New York: Macmillan, 1948), p.126.

ers. They can mourn with them. That is, they can imagine that their entire surroundings know of their suffering, appreciate it, sympathize with them and offer hope and comfort. The spiritual world is also there: they can appeal to it and it can answer, sending a dream or other signs. They can consult with it and seek from it answers to those basic, existential questions which are naturally and spontaneously triggered by the death of a loved one. We can say that this type of universe—social community and spiritual world—fulfills an important inner psychic function, that of "holding," or better still, a "connective function." They help Gilgamesh to re-establish the endangered connection with himself.

The idea of a "connective function" played by the intact social community is of paramount importance. The omnipresence and "omnisentience," if we may call it thus (the completely empathic attitude), of his world centers him, allowing him to connect up with basic aspects of his wider self. Because he knows that his pain is heard and understood, the pain, itself, is confirmed as an important part of himself. Finding echo and approval from the community, powerful emotions in danger of being split off (because of their sheer monumentality), are connected back to the sufferer. And this in turn connects the sufferer back to his wider self. In this way any possible dissociation from his feelings, from his inner world, is healed. And so Gilgamesh, the mourner, is brought back from a potentially solitary position; the risk of dissociation from his feelings, the risk of alienation from himself and from the world is regained.

We can say that Gilgamesh's suffering, although it is definitely deeply felt, is to a certain extent mitigated by his relationship with the men, animals, and nature which make up his universe. They constitute a network of relationships that uphold him, offering security and comfort, creating a highly stable sense of his own identity and value. Furthermore, the gods with whom he lives are *there* for Gilgamesh. He can call upon them and they answer. The omnipresence of the spiritual offers the hope of being able to find a sense of meaning in the seemingly meaningless experience of death.

DEATH TODAY
❧

Few social communities and religious groups offer mourners such comfort today. Jewish ritual, on the decline like most other traditional systems of ritual and meaning, still offers an impressive example of psychological understanding of the plight of mourners. It also bears astounding similarities to the Gilgamesh epic. For example, the tearing of one's garment (which Gilgamesh spontaneously does in his despair) is prescribed for members of the immediate family. A small rip is to be made on the left sleeve. This allows a certain outlet for the expression of grief, frustration, and despair. A clear acting out of grief implies the presence of a social group for whom the gesture has meaning: an echo of sympathy is appealed to and is implicit in the action. The community is called upon to help mourners, especially in the ritual *shiva*. *Shiva* (sitting) lasts for a period of seven days, during which mourners are visited by family and friends who sit and talk with them. The spontaneous refusal to acknowledge the death is granted a certain recognition in the custom of having the tombstone put into place no sooner than one year after the death. Questions about the meaning of life and death, which inevitably plague mourners, are both acknowledged and counteracted by the religion's insistence that one get on with life as soon as possible. Jewish mourners are not allowed to wander through the steppes seeking life because, as soon as the seven days of the *shiva* are over, they are to get on with life. This is one reason why the dead must be buried as soon as possible. The spiritual realm is the frame of reference for the entire ritual. In addition, special prayers are said to accompany the soul of the deceased both during *shiva* and periodically throughout the year. This ritual stresses the omnipresence of God and of the religious community. The solitude of mourners is known to be especially difficult after *shiva* is over, after friends and relatives leave, and life begins again.

Christianity also offers lonely mourners solace: for Christians look forward to meeting the lost loved one in the afterlife. Thus, the painful time of loss and abandonment is limited; it knows bound-aries. Alphonse de Lamartine, the French Romantic poet, well expresses the plight and the hopes of Christian mourners who, in the 19th century, are quite naturally also believing mourners. But first a few preliminary remarks on the poet and his times are necessary. The Romantic period was a time when poets chose solitude, retreat-ing from the masses into their proverbial "ivory towers." Instead of the comfort of a community of social individuals (such as we have seen in the primitive contexts of Gilgamesh and in the Jewish ritual) these poets believed in the comfort of communion with nature. And so, it was here, in isolated bucolic landscapes, that they mused on life and death; they contemplated and sought consolation and spiri-tual elevation in nature. Nature provided them with a suitable atmospheric backdrop for their search for transcendence; its essence was elevating and comforting. But in his poem "L'isolement" ("Solitude"), Lamartine finds no comfort in nature. Written in August 1819, the lines were inspired by the poet's feelings at an espe-cially difficult time of his life, less than a year after the death of his beloved Elvire. Sitting, as he was wont to do, on a mountainside, in the shade of an oak tree, Lamartine looks at the landscape around him. He describes the natural beauties that lie spread out before him and recalls how they used to enchant him. But now, he says:

> *But these sweet scenes o'er my indifferent soul*
> *Can neither peaceful charm nor transport shed.*
> *A wandering spirit on the earth I stroll;*
> *The sun of life no longer warms the dead*

And he goes on to make this statement which most people suffer-ing from the death of a loved one would readily agree with:

> *And I exclaim, joy nowhere waits for me!*

Although he feels completely alone, abandoned, and, hence, joyless, Lamartine finds one important consolation: death. For, in death, he believes, he will find his beloved Elvire again:

And yet, perchance, beyond his sphere may be
Lands, where the true sun lights another sky;
Where, were I once from earthly bondage free,
All I have dreamed so long, would meet mine eye.[4]

The thought of death and, especially, of a life after death, with the hope of meeting the beloved "in the afterlife," offers deep consolation for those who believe.

And so, from the early Babylonian epic to Jewish ritual and the Romantic era, we see examples of the ways in which religious belief and practice attempt to comfort mourners from the solitude they faced at the death of a loved one.

Today this kind of comfort is lacking. In an age of rationalism and deep religious skepticism we cannot turn to the gods or to religious belief. In a period of crumbling social structures, the dependence on a community of support is not such a matter of fact. In a time when nature is often barred from our asphalt cities and emptied of transcendental meaning, it cannot offer elevation or hint at transcendence: its rivers and trees cannot be anthropomorphized into commiserating beings. What remains for us is our own, contemporary canon of belief: knowledge, science, medicine. In times of spiritual need, when we feel alone, abandoned and miserable in the face of death, we more readily turn to the medical doctor than to the priest. He prescribes medicine to help us find the distance we seek from our suffering: it helps subdue and even suppress our unbearable pain. This is our specifically modern and rational "system of belief" which we spontaneously turn to for help and comfort. In the same line of rationale we may also attend seminars and lectures on the subject of death and dying. Here we seek intellectual understanding of the experience of solitude. Consciously, we want to comprehend the experience of death and the solitude it confronts us with. Unconsciously, we often want to rationalize away our unbearable fears and suffering. And so, our method of

---

4. Alphonse de Lamartine, "Solitude," a translation of the French "L'isolement," in *Poetic Meditations*, translated by William North (London: H.G. Clarke, 1848), pp.10-11

approach to the problem is more one of distancing: either we try to buffer our pain through medicine that wraps us as if in cotton wool, or we learn about the experience of death and pain and thus can label and shelve it. I believe, however, that there is another need which modern people seek to fulfill in the seminar setting, and that is the basic archetypal need of sharing and perhaps even of acting out. In such a setting people have a forum in which they can allow themselves to express their deeper feelings about this painful experience. They find a previously unknown but naturally interested and empathic audience with whom they can share this level of their experience. It is amazing that modern people can more readily express deeply personal feelings to "perfect strangers" (as we say) than to kith and kin.

This is what differentiates our suffering from solitude from that of people in an intact culture. We are independent, proud of not needing the community; we are also, however, alone to deal with basic and difficult human problems. The problem of death and dying, and of the suffering of those left behind, belongs to the lot of mankind. As Sadder, the Schenkin who lives in the depths of the ocean, tells Gilgamesh, "When the gods created man, they distributed death to him." And she advises him then to turn back to life and rejoice in it. Unquestioningly a part of his collectively oriented culture, Gilgamesh's relationship to his gods and to his co-believers (fellow men who constitute his social and simultaneously religious community) compensate for the loss of the loving relationship. Held and supported in his personal solitude, Gilgamesh can feel the very sensible presence, the omnipresence, of values and beliefs with which he can identify. *Identify* is the key word here. Living in such a culture, believing in its values and identifying with it and them, definitely helps to re-establish the connection to ourselves, to our own life when it is endangered, for example, by loss, separation and solitude. Our contemporary addiction to individualism, our insistence on freedom of will and thought are in extreme contrast to the Gilgamesh type of culture. The negative side of our modern value system catches up with us in the domain of solitude.

EXILE IN FORMER TIMES
∽

Another experience of solitude has preoccupied human beings since the beginning of time: the solitude caused by banishment or exile. Separation from family, friends, land or culture is so obviously the cause of great pain that it was and still is used as punishment for very serious offenses. Early testimonials tell mainly of exile from land or culture; the bible story of the expulsion from the Garden of Eden is the archetypal model for existential abandonment. Modern testimonials refer more frequently to a different kind of exile, from society in general, in the form of solitary confinement. We shall be looking in detail at mainly two texts here; the first one is ancient—from about three thousand years ago; the second is a contemporary text.

The biblical story of Moses is an impressive tale on the subject of abandonment and potential solitude caused by repeated separations and exiles. Moses is the prototype of an exiled person in a period in time which seems to have been marked by strong cultural and social bonding. His socio-cultural milieu is not dissimilar to Gilgamesh's in its unquestioning acceptance of and reliance on the group, the collective framework. But, the affiliation to people and land is a relatively new phenomenon for the Hebrew people in the story; furthermore, the initial situation is an extremely inimical one. This makes for a great deal more poignancy and drama in the story of Moses and his life.

Moses actually goes through at least four experiences of separation or exile during his lifetime, perhaps even five, if we include his death just outside of the Promised Land. First of all, as everyone knows, Moses is separated from his mother, his family, and his culture soon after birth. The original text[5] says that when he was

---

5. Here, and in all further references to the Bible, I shall be referring to the newest authorized scholarly translation, *The NIV Interlinear Hebrew-English Old Testament,* four volumes in one, *Genesis-Malachi,* edited by John R. Kohlenberger III (Grand Rapids, MI: Zondervan Publishing House, 1979), Exodus, 2:3.

three months old, his mother, a daughter of the tribe of Levi, set him out in a basket. She was trying to save her child's life, for, according to the Pharaoh's edict, as a male Hebrew baby, he would have to be drowned in the river. This first exile—the separation from his biological mother—is of relatively short duration, for soon after being set out in the basket the Pharaoh's handmaidens find Moses and bring him to the Pharaoh's daughter. She realizes that he must be a Hebrew baby; luckily, Moses' sister has observed all of this, and stands by as the Pharaoh's daughter is handed the baby; the sister then offers to get a Hebrew "nursing woman" for the baby. She goes to get his mother to nurse the baby and brings him back to her. We do not know how long Moses was nursed by his mother, but it seems that as soon as he was weaned, his mother brought him back to the Pharaoh's daughter, who then declared him to be her own son and gave him his name, "Moshe," from "*mosheeteehu*" which means "I drew him." She says, "For I drew him out of the waters (*hamayim*)." This is Moses's second separation from his mother, family, and culture, his second exile, and it seems to have been the definitive separation from his mother, for she is never mentioned again in the text. But somehow Moses knows of his Hebrew origins, and this sets the scene for his subsequent exiles.

Moses' third exile is his first voluntary one; he flees the land of Egypt which has become the oppressive home of his people when, as an adult, he happens to see an Egyptian kill a Hebrew slave. He then kills the Egyptian and, fearing for his own life, promptly flees across the border to Midian. He returns to Egypt with one purpose in mind—to leave Egypt once again. This is Moses' second voluntary exile, but actually his fourth. This one has a higher purpose and has been commanded by God in order to lead His people out of slavery in Egypt into the Promised Land. Moses' fifth and final exile has a similar tone to the story of the Garden of Eden. Having caused God to be angry with him, he dies without being allowed to enter the Promised Land. The quality of this final exile is perhaps the most tragic to our eyes. It is, however, interesting to note that none of the exiles or separations is presented in a particularly emotional way.

The early date of this text, thought to have been written around the 12th century B.J.C.E., accounts for the unemotional and seemingly unpsychological account of Moses' repeated exiles from family, friends, culture, and homeland. There is, however, one very telling hint at the pain of the man called Moses. While living in exile in Midian, he marries a woman called Zipporah who then bears him a son; the text says that Moses calls the boy Gershom and explains the name in this way: "For I have become an alien in a foreign land." A father must have suffered quite a bit from his situation to have named his first male baby after this state. Having become an alien in a foreign land must further be understood in context of the times and culture. We can surmise that it was uncomfortable and unpleasant to live in exile, a fact still true today. It was also dangerous, for one never knew how one would be welcomed in the foreign land; shadow projections were generally made onto the foreigners. (Our modern situation bears quite distinct similarities.) And so, becoming a refugee meant exposing oneself to an unforeseeable situation: it could be fraught with problems, difficulties, and also danger. When we try to walk in Moses' shoes, we can imagine this uprooting must have been especially painful for him. He was brought up as a stranger in a strange house, among a strange family which was even the declared enemy of his own family and people. He was abandoned by his real mother, not only once but twice, at three months of age and after weaning. Moses lived and relived his initial uprooting again and again. But his fourth exile, in the company of, and at the head of, his people, can be seen as an important compensation for the initial uprooting.

And here we have the key to Moses' psychic survival from the existential solitude which was potentially his lot since birth: his deep emotional ties to his people and to their God. Moses is obviously held, firmly supported, by this deep and obliging commitment. It provides him with a sense of security, a feeling of meaningfulness, and, hence, a solid sense of his own identity and self-worth. The all-importance of such a support is what makes him capable of risking life and limb again and again for this people and their God, for taking on and carrying out his mission as the leader of his people. He can dare to kill the Egyptian slavedriver, to confront the Pharaoh, to lead the people out of Egypt and to guide them through the Sinai Desert for forty years, all because this commitment is so essential for him. It compensates for the solitude which has been a central aspect of his life since his birth and his raising in the Pharaoh's palace. Ironically, it is this commitment which brings about his fifth and final exile, as I call his exclusion from the Promised Land. Deeply disappointed in the way people cry out for water in the desert, Moses over-reacts, smiting the rock which he knows to hold water, in anger. God punishes him for the anger by denying him the joy of finally entering into the land of Israel: he is to die within sight of the land, but is not allowed to enter. From a psychological point of view, Moses' anger is all too understandable. It has to do with the importance which his people have had for him. Had they not been so important to him, he would not have become so disappointed or so angry with them. But God is adamant in His condemnation of violence.

Entering the Promised Land could have brought Moses a final and absolute reunion and reconciliation with the homeland, the maternal element. But his fate as an uprooted person, again and again ejected into the role of an outsider with neither a mother nor a maternal land, seems to condemn him to a deep, even an unfathomable solitude. Moses finds a satisfying role and position in life because of his spiritual and social commitment. Feeling at one with his people, he *belongs* to a social and religious community. And this belonging provides him with a new and powerful sense of not being alone and abandoned. And so, despite these repeated separations, despite his having felt himself to be "a stranger in a strange land," Moses does not flounder. From the viewpoint of depth psychology we would describe Moses' "case" in the following way. Separated from his mother at an early age, he grew up in a foreign culture; this was deeply unsettling. As compensation, he became a socially and politically committed person. This commitment made him feel at home in his skin and in the world. One could say that through it, he found a home for himself in the world. In this way he was saved from experiencing the otherwise necessarily severe and disturbing effects of existential solitude.

THE CONNECTIVE FUNCTION
OF THE SOCIO-SPIRITUAL UNIVERSE
IN FORMER TIMES

❧

Before going on to examine more modern examples of solitude, I want to summarize what we have seen in these early texts. Both are from periods in history where the social group was extremely important for the individual. The individual was embedded in the group and very much a part of it; separation from it was dangerous—even physically dangerous. When, as in Gilgamesh's case, the individual is alone, for example because of the death of a loved one, he is never completely alone: the sense of belonging to a social and spiritual community is so strong that the group can actually act as a reinforcement of the tie to oneself, to life in general, and to the world at large. Moses, separated from his group, finds it again and commits himself and his life to it completely. He become its leader in a time of dire need. He becomes the hero, the champion of the group, whose faith is not easily shaken. Moses has actually no existence outside the group: one cannot imagine his life without it once he has pledged to lead the group out of Egypt. Moses lives for and with, because of, and through this community. We realize now the extent to which he depends on it for the justification of his own existence.

The stories of Gilgamesh and Moses show us that solitude definitely was a part of earlier cultures. But this was a relative solitude, readily remedied by the surrounding society. In order to try to imagine the kind of situation in which early people lived we can think of symbiotic families today. In such groups, when, for example, one of the adult children is faced with solitude because of a child's leaving home or a spouse's death, the suffering is sensed by the entire family which quasi-automatically rushes in to fill up the gap. The members of the family all spontaneously co-operate to try to help the person. On the one hand, there is definitely comfort offered by the group. On the other hand, people today can feel the group's spontaneous reaction as interference, even meddling in their affairs. This type of reaction is more typical of modern people and their developmental situation, with its stress on independence and individualism. It is very unlikely that people of earlier periods experienced this rushing to the fore of the family or the community as interference. It was just what happened; it was natural and normal and it was even expected by all concerned.

The other side of the omnipresent and omnisentient group (and naturally of the symbiotic family or community today) is the fact that it implied and even demanded conformity. One's identity, validity and worth was guaranteed—there was no question of alienation from oneself or from the group—as long as one complied with the group and its values. For example, people living in small rural communities today still have much to tell about such situations: as long as one complies, approval and support are forthcoming, But one must not, for example, disagree with the prevalent opinions of the Church, the favored teacher, or the popular mayor. There is little or no tolerance for individual's opinions. In this way such a community group does stand in the way of the development of individuals.

EXILE AND
SOLITARY CONFINEMENT TODAY
·◇·

Today the punishment of exile is still practiced as a means of keeping people in check. Exile from one's country is relatively rare at the end of the 20th century. It was, however, a painful reality in the not too distant past, as we know from the seemingly voluntary exile of the Jews and the political opponents to Nazism. Robert Musil who sought exile in Switzerland, suffered so from this situation that he described it thus. On January 20, 1942, three months before his death, exile meant to him suffering like a buffalo whose powerful horns have been replaced by painful corns, as he then said:

Imagine a buffalo who suddenly develops painful corns
where he used to have tremendous horns. This being—
with its extraordinary forehead that once sported
arms—this is the man in exile.[6]

Exile in the form of imprisonment, even of solitary confinement, is
a still a painful reality for people the world over who commit serious offenses against their respective societies. Noteworthy is the
universality of this form of punishment: it must be especially
painful or it must be imagined as such, otherwise it would not be
so widespread throughout the world *and* throughout time. Many
accounts of the suffering from this type of solitude exist today. We
can mention Arthur Koestler's *Darkness at Noon* and Oriana
Fallaci's *A Man*.[7] Both novels are about a central figure who is kept
in solitary confinement because of political beliefs and activities.
Both of these figures attempt to avoid their terrible feelings of solitude by cultivating relationships—relationships with almost anything they find. Rubashov, in Koestler's novel, spends most of his
time and energy worrying about and feeling his toothache, and
reminiscing about his political past. His ties to his own history and
to his physical pain help him retain his sense of feeling related.
These memories and sensations help him keep a sense of who he is,
help him re-establish a connection to himself and to his life, so seriously endangered by the solitude of his confinement. They make
him feel related to himself, give him a sense of who he is, just as
Gilgamesh's dream and Moses' commitment to his people did.

   Oriana Fallaci tells the story of another political prisoner,
Alekos Panagoulis. The story of the all too brief, but very intense,
relationship this prisoner cultivates with a bug provides interesting
insights into what it means to feel related. The example is especially valuable for our reflections on the relationships people keep
with animals, and about relationships in general. Implicitly we dis-

---

6. "Why don't you read his great novel; April 15th is the 50th anniversary of the
death of the Austrian author Robert Musil," by Wolf Scheller, in *Jüdisch Allgemeine
Zeitung*, No. 47 (April 9, 1992), p. 15. Translation mine.
7. Arthur Koestler, *Darkness at Noon* (New York: Bantam, 1984); and Oriana
Fallaci: *A Man*, William Weaver, trans. (New York: Simon & Schuster, 1980).

cover here what it means when we do not feel related, when we feel alone.

In the novel, Panagoulis is shown in all the varied ways he tries to assuage his suffering in lengthy solitary confinement: he reads books, tries to learn a new language. We could say that he cultivates a relationship to culture, or perhaps even to his own mental faculties. Then, one day he finds a bug in his cell. His state of mind, his mood, is drastically affected: life becomes worth living again. Panagoulis feels once again connected in a positive way to himself and his life. But let us see how Panagoulis experiences it in his own words. When he notices the bug, he calls out to it, asking it to come to him. He pats it, wondering all the while how long this "company" can last: how long does a bug live? How long will he live? And he recalls how, as a little boy, he tried to tame a scarab. At that time in his life he enjoyed having someone to talk to who would not scold him. He decides to name this new companion Salvador Dali, because of his antennae. And he imagines confiding in Dali, telling him how frightened he really is. And so we see how the bug becomes not only *like* a real person: it even takes on the very important role of a confessor, or of a confident: this infinitesimal and otherwise totally insignificant "pest" becomes, in the mind of the prisoner, a human being or rather some kind of animate and empathic being to whom he can entrust his most secret thoughts, and especially his fears. This imaginative leap jolts Panagoulis into another state of mind: he reflects on the difference the presence and the *friendship* of the bug makes to him:

> Suddenly . . . thanks to a tiny creature which at other times would only have disgusted you, you realized you wanted to live, and after all, you can live also in a cell of nine paces by seven.

And not only can he imagine living again, he can rejoice in the idea. He says:

> You only need a cot, a table, a chair, a flush toilet, and a cockroach. And maybe a few books, some paper, a couple of pencils.

But this incomparable fellowship comes to a cruel end when a guard enters the prisoner's cell. Panagoulis warns him to be careful not to step on Dali, but the guard crushes Dali with his foot. And Panagoulis' feelings for himself are dashed in one moment. The bug has already become human: he imagines how it cries out in pain: it is as if a "being with arms and legs" has been killed: "It brought back to you the awareness of your solitude."[8]

This thought "made the blood rush to [his] head." Panagoulis becomes so enraged that he attacks the murderous guard and all the other guards who then rush into his cell. As a result, the conditions of his solitary confinement are reinforced: he is to have no more letters, nor paper, pen, or books, and he must wear handcuffs day and night. The lonely prisoner's desperate reaction on being deprived of his newly found friend ironically results in more extreme conditions of isolation.

WHAT IT MEANS TO FEEL RELATED/ISOLATED

·∽·

This passage about a man's short-lived but intense relationship with a bug gives us a good idea of what it means to feel related, and, hence, what the lack of such feelings—what solitude—is actually all about. When we feel related, we feel an empathic connection to another. This means on one level that we imagine, we have the feeling or the impression, that the other feels for or sympathizes with us. This "other" appears to us as an empathic listener, open and sympathetic to our secret plans and ideas, ready and willing to understand our emotional plight. Panagoulis imagines telling the bug of his fears.

But an empathic relationship is a two-way thing. As this text so well shows, another important aspect of our need for an empath-

---

8. This, and the text quoted above, are from Oriana Fallaci's *A Man*, pp. 74-75.

ic other is our need to have a place to invest our own positive feelings: we need objects for our feelings of approval, admiration, and
empathy, perhaps just as much as we need to feel that we are the
object of such feelings. Panagoulis feels *for* the bug, thinking of,
and imagining its pain and suffering, and sharing it. This is the
other, less frequently spoken of level of the empathic relationship:
the other becomes the object of our tenderness, of our affection. I
believe that this is a major point. It means that positive fantasies
about the other and about consensus with this positive other also
make up our deepest yearnings for relationship. When we have an
appropriate object for these fantasies, then we can feel related to,
connected to, ourselves and to life, even in the most arduous of cir-
cumstances. Life becomes worth living.

One could say in a rather neutral, "nothing but" kind of way,
that the presence of another with whom we feel related merely provides us with a projection screen. We have a place to invest these
positive feelings that we need to feel. (But actually we can only see
in the other what we need to and are capable of seeing. Probably
we all, to a certain extent, also need a projection screen for negative feelings and fantasies, and therefore, also get involved in very
difficult relationships. They enable us to feel, and even to express,
more difficult parts of ourselves, more negative feelings.) When we
have no appropriate place to invest our positive fantasies, then we
can lose all interest in life. We can lose the connection to our innermost being: a deep sense of solitude is a state close to death. To mix
metaphors a bit, when we feel related, echo becomes possible, and
without some degree of echo we do not feel whole.

Panagoulis' example also makes us realize how important
animals can be. Scientific research has even proven this to be true
in the post-operative healing process. Patients in American hospi-
tals who were allowed to pat their domestic animals after serious
operations recovered more quickly than the sample group who
was not allowed this opportunity. We also know how many older
people today, otherwise living in relative isolation, cultivate an
intense relationship with an animal—a cat, a dog, even a bird. The
beloved animal becomes invested with distinct personality traits
and receives a great deal of love. We can imagine now how this
relationship can actually be a lifeline to the person's self, reviving

the sense of joy in life itself. Adolescents, too, often tend to invest a lot of energy in relationships to animals, whether it be to the family dog or cat, to horses, or even to stray animals. During a period in its life when the child is shy or awkward in human relationships, it can actually cultivate a relationship to itself through its relating to the animal. Everyone has heard more pathological versions of the same, of eccentric loners who avoid people, but who live in intimacy with animals. All of these examples show how important it is to feel related and what feeling related, even if it is only to an animal, can mean for the person. From this we can surmise that part of what makes solitude so painful is the lack of the projection screen, the lack of an object for fantasies and feelings, many of which revolve around sharing, concern, understanding, empathy, consensus, and acceptance. We need a place to feel positive feelings just as much as we need the empathy we fantasize coming from the other.

The relationship between Panagoulis and the bug is all too relevant today. It is characteristic of modern life that the ties to a larger whole (to a socio-spiritual community) such as we have seen in the examples of Gilgamesh and Moses, are not a matter of fact. The presence of such ties can help compensate for the desperation that a person faced with solitude can feel. But the situation today is generally very different. Each one of us must find the relationship that can comfort us at the moment. It may be a relationship with a group of friends, with an animal, or even with a computer. For us today, as we shall be seeing soon, one aspect is of fundamental importance: the internalization of a positive early experience in relating. This is what makes us capable of relationship. Unfortunately, such experiences are often lacking.

SOLITUDE IN MODERN TIMES

⟿

Our situation today is quite different from that of our forefathers. Few today believe in a spiritual world, many live "as strangers in a strange land." With the heavens empty and nature banished from our urban environment, the fan-

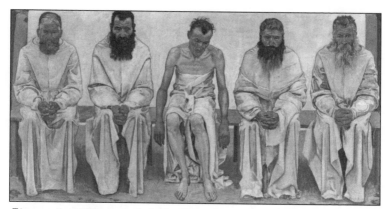

Figure 1. "Weary of Life," Ferdinand Hodler (1853-1918). Munich: Neue Pinakothek.

tasy of a commiserating nature is dead for many people. Solitude is a subject of concern to an extent it never before has been in the history of mankind. And it promises to become an even more frequent motive for desperation and desperate acts in the future. Solitude is more threatening than ever before because it is actually more solitary than ever before.

The subject has been broached mainly in connection with the aged. Older people are not the only ones to suffer from loneliness today. Far from it. But it is permissible—it is not embarrassing—to speak of this problem in the case of old people. The aged have no place in our world, neither in our image of what a human being is, nor in our physical living conditions. Youth is the dominant image of our times. Any positive characteristics associated with age—for example, wisdom of life and politics—are associated with ancient history. People no longer part of the work force are often even physically exiled. Living conditions in modern cities, with their small apartments, make it difficult to integrate the aged. In simple terms, families no longer have the space to put up a grandparent. There are, of course, psychological dimensions to the problem as well. On the one hand, people have the need to proclaim loudly and live according to their own individuality. This often means living alone or at least living with only the nuclear family. On the other hand, old age is definitely a kind of shadow which we try to deny for as long as possible; therefore, we keep any reminders of it out of mind and out of sight. Shutting out any references to age helps us create the illusion of never having to become old and wrinkled, weak or sick. In this respect it is also a paradoxical loneliness that we try to shut out because the aged are often left alone, without a partner. So we shut out the image of solitude which is also unacceptable, but create at the same time more solitude for the aged.

I would like to examine one aspect of modern solitude in more detail: that stemming from demographic developments. Demographic developments of the 20th century have led to the exile and isolation of entire groups of people, therefore blowing the contemporary problem of solitude into epidemic proportions. The lack of space in our cities is only one aspect of these developments. Basic changes within society involve huge masses of people throughout the world. Since at least the end of the 19th century we have been able to observe the fate of immigrant populations, fleeing their homelands because of economic desperation and political oppression, two factors which often go hand in hand. Furthermore, we observe in more recent times tidal waves of homeless people: amazing numbers of people who do not opt for living in the streets (like the rare vagabonds before them), but are forced to live on the streets of many modern cities. Having lost their homes because of financial problems, they are relegated to the street and depend on charity in order to survive. We can merely cringe at the thought of what all of this will mean for the future. The fact is that both the homeless and the immigrant populations present modern society with an immense population of uprooted people, people lacking any ties to the social and cultural community within whose boundaries they just happen to live. Their plight will become a major problem in years to come.

It is actually since the end of the 19th century that cities have become the dwelling place of those uprooted from their familiar (family and habitual) surroundings. The beginning of the industrial age saw the first migratory waves of people in search of economic betterment. But, in leaving their rural homes, the first industrial workers also left their ties to a community (family, friends, neighbors—a whole social network) and to a system of values (a homogeneous and reliable cultural and religious background).

The Urban Work Force Versus the Tribal Lap

∾·

We can picture what urban solitude might have been like in its early manifestations in Degas' *Ironing Woman*. Here we see a typical city worker and dweller. She is a person who, in order to earn a living, does a job with more or less devotion and energy, but without feeling a deep emotional attachment, either to the work, or to her employer, or to those for whom the ironing is accidentally being done. The idea of having an "emotional connection" to a job may even sound strange to us today. What is that all about? We can comprehend the lack of connection of the urban worker to his or her job best in contradistinction to what I call living and working in the tribal lap. When a tribesman built a canoe, he did it in an exactly prescribed manner— most likely even as his father had taught him to, and as his father's father had taught his father to, etc., down the succeeding generations. And building the canoe was an important activity whose meaning and significance was quite clear for its builder. Not only was all of this obviously purposeful and meaningful activity— work—it was also a sacred act, or an act sanctified in some way. Prayers would be chanted during the building, or when it was done, when the canoe would be dedicated to the gods. In these various ways, work, for our "primitive" forefathers took place within a meaningful social and religious framework. It was part of a tradition and had a definite meaning for the person and the group of which he felt a part.

In contrast, Degas' *Ironing Woman* is most likely ironing for someone she does not even know or may never even have seen. Her spiritual ties, if, indeed, she still has any, are to a completely

Figure 2. "The Ironing Woman," Edgar Degas (1834-1917). Munich: Bayerische Staatsgemäldesammlung.

different world. This world is separate from her job, has nothing to do with it. If she is lucky enough to get a sabbath day of rest from work, she can pursue her spiritual commitment then. Furthermore, she did not necessarily learn ironing from her mother and her work has certainly no deeper, historic background in her own life or in the life of her community. She performs this work in order to earn money. If there is anything at all meaningful about the work it is this material recompense. The work is otherwise devoid of any feeling relationship. It does not offer a projection screen for the woman's own feelings or values. It does not reinforce her connection to herself, even as a pet dog might have. It does not make her feel anchored in her reality, or in touch with a vital part of herself.

Such is the situation of modern city workers and dwellers. The lack of a feeling of relatedness—to a community of people and to its values—is the predominant socio-cultural background of our times. The lack of a connection to nature, which became extreme toward the second half of the 20th century, is slowly being replaced by a growing concern for the destruction of nature through the tools of industry and the race toward Progress. Our eminently anonymous devotion to life and work among and for people we hardly know, with no omnipresent deities, makes for the epidemic proportions of solitude in our world. But it also makes our solitude particularly hopeless. There is no comfort from friends, relatives, nature, or from the gods. This phenomenon is so well known that it hardly need be dwelt on here.

Modern Uprooting and Ersatz Pleasures for Relationships

⌀·

Perhaps one further point should be mentioned, although it is more typical of the American scene. Here, even within the city, repeated uprooting is a relatively common way of life. People tend to move not only from city to city, but also from one neighborhood to the other; as their present neighborhood becomes more predominantly African-American, Hispanic, Jewish, Oriental, or other immigrant population, those who can afford to move on. Again and again entire families leave their habitual surroundings, the community which has become familiar, even significant, for them. The society with which they have come to relate and even identify must be exchanged for another. Such a situation causes serious problems, most obviously for the children who, having to change schools and find new friends, find themselves again and again in the role of outsiders. Being an outsider means being excluded, feeling alone and lonely. The psychic stress of being exposed to such feelings at an early age can be extremely trying and even destabilizing.

But modern research has shown that children can recover from their experiences relatively quickly.[9] And, parenthetically speaking, exposure to the role of being outsiders helps people identify with outsiders. This can reduce the likelihood that these people will reject foreign elements within their society. People who have known what such an experience is like are less prone to be cruel or even violent, for example, toward foreign immigrant populations. It is precisely this kind of model experience which is lacking in European urban environments, thus making violence toward refugees, foreign workers, and minority groups easier to perpetrate. The experiential identification model is missing in the perpetrator's repertoire of life situations. While American children learn to be more accepting of strangers, their repeated uprooting often makes them "strangers in a strange land" emotionally.

The plight of women who stay at home is actually worse when the family gets uprooted. These women do not have an institutionalized opportunity for meeting other people in their new environment. The only advantage they have over their children in dealing with solitude is that of age. This may mean that they have the maturity to deal with this stress in a more adequate manner; that is, it need not necessarily destabilize the mother as easily as it does the children. Nonetheless, there are women who crack under the stress of this situation: at home alone for long periods of time, they feel lonely and helpless, and turn, for example, to alcohol to relieve their distress. The statistics on alcoholism among women have been on the rise for some time now.

---

9. Letitia A. Peplau and Daniel Perlman, *Loneliness, A Sourcebook of Current Theory, Research and Therapy* (New York: John Wiley & Sons, 1982).

Figure 3. "Drunk Woman Drowsing," Pablo Picasso (1881-1973). Kunstmuseum, Bern, Stiftung Othmar Huber Collection.

But alcoholism is only one of the ersatz activities which modern life offers to the lonely. Not only in America, but all over the civilized world, one finds similar compensatory activities, meant to grant the lonely a sense of home, of comfort, of company. Television, video movies, recorders, computer games, drug and alcohol abuse, even shopping, and just plain keeping busy are among the activities which enable the solitary to keep their suffering under control. These activities help numb feelings of worthlessness and meaninglessness which are part of the experience. Especially among the young, criminality is on the rise as a means of counteracting the solitude of cities. The "gang" offers its members a sense of belonging: its escapades weld the members together in a peer group of shared values, pitted against "the others." And when a sense of community and shared values is lacking, it is much easier to perform criminal acts: the people who are hurt "just happen" to be one's neighbors.

The lack of a community also means the lack of a place of meeting. And this has led to the development of entire industries intent on selling pleasures to the lonely. The partner-finding institutions are blooming, whether they depend on letters, photographs, newspapers, or computers. Various forms of prostitution have increased, be they imports from third world countries, or call girl and escort organizations. Peoples' needs for companionship have remained despite the fact that the communities have become dissociated. The sexual needs of the lonely are there and need to be fulfilled, lest they lead to the witch hunts of the past when evil intentions and, especially, destructiveness were the crimes witches were accused of; meanwhile it was the secret wishes of the prosecutors that were projected onto the unfortunate women.

Edward Hopper's paintings of American cities are often seen as accurate illustrations of the solitude that characterizes life in the big city. The cold light embracing the isolated figures in these paintings is, however, according to the artist himself, more an effort at reproducing certain types of light. Interesting though that our images of city life are so strong that we can hardly believe the painter's perspective. Distance and separateness, individualism and also solitude belong to our image of what modern life is about.

Hopper also shows a predilection for such motifs—of people alone or at least very separate from each other, generally in a city backdrop; it was just such figures that he chose to put into the kind of light he was interested in painting. But we all know that this is an all too black and cold image of city life. Many cities and neighborhoods within cities have relatively little violence. But a major cause for violence in cities is definitely the lack of community and of shared values.

The only hope for the future which I foresee is the revival of community and spirituality. The example of the United States at the end of the 19th century shows the extent to which immigrant peoples tended to hold fast to their religious customs and beliefs. Such a tendency could help counteract the crumbling social structures and the sense of isolation which are the lot of the uprooted in the cities. The city as *locus par excellence* for the experience of solitude is, however, only one isolating aspect of modern life.

THE CRUMBLING OF SOCIAL STRUCTURES AND THE LACK OF CONNECTION TO ONESELF: NARCISSISM

～

The crumbling of social structures is a stage of development which seems to belong to the advance of civilization and the development of the individual human psyche. It goes hand in hand with an uprise of individualism which, in itself, seems to preclude strong and reliable social structures. The number of people living alone is greater than ever before in history. Families are deteriorating, people are choosing not to marry or not to live together; they are deciding to separate, to divorce. The so-called "Singles' Society" is on the rise. The extended family has long been a thing of the past, but even nuclear

Figure 4. "Nighthawks," by Edward Hopper (1882-1967), oil on canvas, 1942. Friends of American Art Collection, 1942.51. Photograph ©1996, The Art Insitute of Chicago.

families are becoming a precarious unit, for single parent families are becoming more and more common.

If, as we have seen in our examples of the past, the socio-spiritual universe used to provide a connective function for its members, then, in times when such a society no longer exists, how is this connective function fulfilled? The answer is too often that it is not fulfilled, or it is not very well fulfilled. Crumbling social structures seem to be, at least in part, responsible for the epidemic proportions of narcissism in our day and age. Narcissism, or the problem of an unstable sense of self-esteem, seems (from our present-day perspective) to stem from lacks or deficiencies. Some people who experience low self-esteem deeply and painfully say they feel they have "holes." They feel a lack in the sense of who they are, a lack of the sense of meaningfulness of life; they feel a lack of understanding from others; they feel alone, abandoned, unloved, misunderstood, unseen, unheard. It is no wonder then that they are extremely sensitive to criticism and constantly seek reassurance of their worth, without ever getting the feeling of having enough. The need to achieve in order to prove their worth to themselves and to others replaces any matter-of-fact sense of self (which seems to have belonged to earlier cultures). But the vicious circle begins here: people who are so concerned about their own worth cannot offer much empathy to others (or to themselves for that matter), so the lack of supportive social structures, the lack of stable relationships which bolster a sense of self is undermined again. And the problem is passed on from generation to generation.

In retrospect the extended family seems to have offered the possibility of multiple reliable relationships. One would, therefore, imagine that the family members were less exposed to solitude. They certainly knew less physical isolation—from another perspective they actually "enjoyed less privacy"—but their suffering from inner solitude through uncaring relationships was, I believe, just as difficult. The advantage of the extended family lay in the possibility it offered of finding, among a multitude of various possible relationships, at least one or some few relationships in which one felt understood and supported.

Speaking of extended families in this way reminds me of a patient who came from a large rural family. The family motto was work, work, work. There was no room for anything else: there was no care taken for anyone's feelings. Life was arranged with very pragmatic considerations and with little care paid to anyone's feeling preferences. For example, my patient was made to sleep with a cousin in a neighboring house when he was 2 years old because his mother was busy with the new baby. This meant that he was torn away from the warmth of the family nest every evening, put to bed by an aunt whom he did not like, and was taken back to his parents' house only at lunchtime the next day. Protest as he would, my patient found no listening or understanding ear for his feelings. He became a very timid person, always uncertain of his own self-worth. It seems as if the basis necessary for a stable sense of self-esteem was missing. And this despite the fact that there was definitely no sign of a deterioration in the social structure of his tight-ly-knit extended family. What seems to have influenced him the most markedly from his strong extended family situation was the importance of obligations to the family. As an adult he shied away from any relationships which might make him obliged to do and care for others.

The deeper emotional and psychological problems of our times are intimately connected with this specific aspect of solitude. Feeling unrelated to our innermost self stems from (and also leads to) feeling unrelated to our fellow human beings—to family, neigh-borhood, culture. And this is exactly what differentiates our mod-ern experiences of solitude from that of our ancestors. Primitive people could always count on some kind of deeper connection—to the gods, to nature, and to the community. We are more absolute-ly alone and suffer accordingly. The separation from our loved ones through death and exile has always been a trying aspect of human life. But never before in the history of mankind have the nets which support us—religion and society—been so frail and unreliable.

THE CONNECTIVE FUNCTION OF RELIABLE AND POSITIVE INNER IMAGES
❧

We have discussed some of the many aspects of the connective function in the examples above, especially in the story of Panagoulis and the bug. The English poet William Cowper, who lived from 1731 until 1800, in his poem titled "Alone" (reproduced on page 38), fantasizes the inner mono-logue of Alexander Selkirk, the man who served as the model for Robinson Crusoe. The poet describes his solitude, speaking of its characteristic traits and bemoaning his fate. But let us look at the stanzas one by one.

Alone

·〇·

I am monarch of all I survey,
My right there is none to dispute;
From the centre all round to the sea,
I am lord of the fowl and the brute.
O Solitude! where are the charms
That sages have seen in thy face?
Better dwell in the midst of alarms
Than reign in this horrible place.

I am out of humanity's reach,
I must finish my journey alone.
Never hear the sweet music of speech,
I start at the sound of my own.
The beasts that roam over the plain
My form with indifference see;
They are so unacquainted with man,
Their tameness is shocking to me.

Society, friendship and love,
Divinely bestowed upon man,
O, had the wings of a dove,
How soon would I taste you again!
My sorrows I then might assuage,
In the ways of religion and truth,
Might learn from the wisdom of age,
And be cheer'd by the sallies of youth.

Religion! what treasure untold
Lies hid in that heavenly word!
More precious than silver or gold,
Or all that this earth can afford.

But the sound of the church-going bell,
These valleys and rocks never heard,
Never sigh'd at the sound of a knell,
Or smiled when a sabbath appear'd.

Ye winds that have made me your sport,
Convey to this desolate shore
Some cordial, endearing report
Of a land I shall visit no more.
My friends, do they now and then send
A wish or a thought after me?
O, tell me I yet have a friend,
Though a friend I am never to see.

How fleet is a glance of the mind!
Compar'd with the speed of its flight,
The tempest himself lags behind
And the swift-winged arrows of light.
When I think of my own native land,
In a moment I seem to be there;
But, alas! recollection at hand
Soon hurries me back to despair.

But the sea-fowl is gone to her nest,
The best is laid down in his lair;
Even here is a season of rest,
And I to my cabin repair.
There's mercy in every place,
And mercy, encouraging thought,
Gives even affliction a grace,
And reconciles man to his lot.[10]

10. William Cowper, "Alone," in Louis Untermeyer, ed.: *Albatross Book of Verse* (London: Collins, 1960). This poem was supposed to have been written by Alexander Selkirk, from the island of Juan Fernandez.

In the first stanza the imagined Selkirk, stranded as we know he is on a deserted island, mentions the charms of solitude and the fact that others have praised these charms. Although one is "monarch of all [one] surveys," Selkirk nevertheless finds the situation "horrible." But the statement is an interesting one for us. It implies that when solitude is chosen, it can be felt as positive, perhaps just because one is lord of all one sees. Living in a self-chosen realm, one is without company, but also without contradiction. Everything one says and does is right, unchallenged. Selkirk, however, whose solitude is not chosen—and this is the essential point here—says that he would prefer to "dwell in the midst of alarms" rather than live in such an unchallenged solitary position.

In the next stanza, the poet goes on to sketch out the kind of social situation he yearns for, speaking of the details of human intercourse which he is missing. And he imagines that he "must finish [his] journey alone." This is definitely one painful aspect of a solitary existence. Although we all die alone (perhaps this is one of the reasons why the fantasy of death is so difficult for us), the person who lives alone has neither family nor friends with whom to part, in whom he or she can seek consolation or comfort. This may be one source of the tradition of calling upon priests, preachers, or rabbis at the moment of death; religion, which is a socially established way of dealing with our deepest needs, realizes our yearning for contact with a caring human being at this final moment of life. The next lines go on to speak of the suffering from a lack of echo in solitude. Being "out of humanity's reach" also means not being able to hear other voices: "never [to] hear the sweet music of speech" and also not to feel empathy from others. The beasts of the plain, his only companions here, react with indifference at the sight of him. This lack of echo, of emotional reactions, is one of the central characteristics which make solitude so painful. Panagoulis showed us this quite plainly. There is no one there who can listen to us, feel with us, no one who even tries to understand us, our words and the feelings which lie behind them.

In the third stanza, the man calls to mind the details of social intercourse which he direly feels missing. "Society, friendship and love" seem to him gifts "bestowed" by God on humanity, but gifts of which he cannot partake. Obviously Cowper is thinking of a very intact society: young and old are both part of the scene. For he could "learn from the wisdom of age" and be "cheer'd by the sallies of youth," as he says. But men and women are only one aspect of this intact setting he yearns for: religion is the other. This description of the religion lacking out in the wilderness makes us realize what religion offers to the socialized individual. In very subtle ways, which we hardly remark otherwise, religion provides a framework granting meaning to our lives and a sense of security. It also makes out of the wilderness a social environment, a civilization. And, it is precisely when one is deprived of these things we otherwise take for granted that one is in a position to realize what and how much they signify. From this we can surmise what those of us who know it can only readily assent to: periodic moments of solitude can help us appreciate more fully whatever we otherwise take for granted. "Absence makes the heart grow fonder," is the rather banal way this has been formulated in the past. Religion is for Selkirk, a man of quite another day and age, a "treasure untold," "more precious than silver and gold." He regrets not being able to hear the church bells, not even the knell. Nor can he appreciate the sabbath and smile "when [it] appears." Bells announcing church services mark the hours of the day for the faithful and for others. In this way the presence of the divine is impressed upon those living within a Christian world. For the Moslems, of course, the same function is served by the muezzins calling out for prayers from the minaret. Time is marked by religious observance (that is, its sacredness is stated); bells or muezzins periodically remind the faithful of this sacral context of life throughout the day. In this way the spiritual frame of reference and the connection to it is subtly, or perhaps even bluntly recalled. Selkirk deeply feels the lack of such reminders of transcendence on his desert island.

He next calls to mind his own personal world of reference, his friends. This stanza is devoted to the importance of inner images of those whom one cherishes. Although, at first, the memory of his friends is consoling, he wonders if these friends also think of him sometime, if they "now and then send a wish or a thought after" him. Once again, here we are reminded of the importance of echoing in our fantasy of relationships. But even the consoling thought of friends makes him desperate, for he is always shaken back to the truth of his reality: the friends are not there. This is an interesting point, which is central to any understanding of solitude. Feeling held by inner images refers to the capacity for holding fast onto memories, imagoes, inner images or simply representations—of those we love. If we can hold onto such inner images, we are less plagued by feelings of loneliness and abandonment when some kind of physical separation takes place. The loved ones remain there in a certain way. The age-old tradition of carrying keepsakes, pictures, and portraits of absent loved ones shows that we often need a little bit of help in the form of certain concrete, physical reminders, to help reinforce the presence of these cherished inner images. In the second-to-last stanza Selkirk bemoans his own unsatisfactorily anchored images. He can think of his native land; he can even vividly imagine being there: "In a moment I seem to be there." But, as he cries out, "alas! recollection at hand Soon hurries me back to despair." This sudden and unexpected realization—being torn back to reality after having lost oneself in fantasies, wishes and memories of happiness—is extremely painful. Remember Panagoulis who suddenly lost all of his recently retrieved joy in living when the guard crushed his bug, thus putting to a cruel end his fantasies of friendship.

The final stanza is devoted to the search for consolation. Selkirk thinks of evening when all beings, even the wild animals on his island, go back to their lair. This is the only mercy offered to him—sleep, which he fittingly calls "a season of rest." This solace is well known to the depressive, who often seek and sometimes find in it a relief from their suffering. Medication often functions in a similar way, dulling one to the pains of reality, making it seem distant and unreal, as if smothered in cotton wool.

Solitude, involuntary solitude at least, appears in this poem as a suffering from various absences—the absence of other beings from whom one can expect empathy along with the absence of more diverse company—that offered by an empathic nature and that of concerned divinities. The empty skies of this desert island are like empty rooms which one enters with a sinking feeling; one hears no echoes here, except that of one's own solitary footsteps. There are two ways in which a feeling can be calmed: either by sleep, when one loses consciousness and cannot realize one's suffering, or by a sense that one is, despite all appearances, not really all alone.

In Cowper's poem we learn something vitally important about what can make the basic, human experience of solitude so painful: the poet's inner images lack in strength or, more precisely, in steadfastness. As he says, when he calls up the images of his friends he feels good, but suddenly his ties to them are broken and he realizes that he is alone. His inner images fail him in important moments: they are unreliable. This we can take to mean that his grounding in himself is unstable. Strong, reliable and supportive inner images help provide a vital connection to oneself. They carry on the empathic contact with one's own self, despite the fact that one may really live in a solitary situation for some time, and contacts in the outer world may be momentarily lacking. Relationships to others in the outer world may be temporarily absent or frail, even be on the verge of crumbling, nevertheless, the sinking feeling of losing all, one's self and one's joy in life, is countered by an unswerving sense of being in contact with one's self. These inner images can then be compared to Gilgamesh's contact with his world and Moses' relationship with his people: they can be called internalizations of such connections. Strong inner images can provide such a sense of being held, making one feel so secure that one in no way suffers, although one is physically truly alone. Cowper's poem is at the same time a very personal revelation of its author's own, personal problem with solitude; it reflects Cowper's own psychological makeup. However, it also is quite exemplary. Most often it is just such a problem that characterizes most people's reaction to solitude.

Schools of depth psychology are very interested in these inner images, which they suppose are formed during early childhood. On the one hand, it seems that the experience of a constantly and consistently caring person who communicates a sense of love, empathy, and security is an important building-block for this central, inner image. The mother is generally considered responsible for the establishment of this foundation. On the other hand, the milieu in general—nature, society, close friends and relatives, the weather and nutrition—plays an important role in the making up this specific foundation for the developing personality.

Jungian psychology especially appreciates the importance of the situation into which the child is born. The real mother can be reliable and fulfill her role of "good enough mother" in a satisfactory manner. But if the child is born into a situation of strife, instability, war or famine, or with a health problem, then this natal milieu is in an important way not dependable and stable. In fairy tale terms we would say that all of the "fairy godmothers" who were invited may have blessed the child. But if one of them is left out and feels rejected, she can place a curse on the child that can seriously hinder its development. In this way, for example, major marital problems of parents, or an uncaring father who mistreats the mother, can be just as responsible for a child's insecurity as an unsatisfactory mother. We then say that there is a problem in the realm of the Great Mother. Mother Nature which can nurture and hold when all goes well, can be just as cruel and destructive when, for example, the child falls ill. Then, the real mother can try as she will, the general situation is deficient. And, in this way it can come to pass that a baby whose mother is attentive, caring, and loving can still become an adult with a serious lack in this domain of reliable and positive inner images because of the situation into which it was born.

I am thinking in this connection of a patient whose relationship to the mother was good and who actually felt that her mother was a "good enough" mother. But, born at the end of the Second World War, the child knew the flight from Eastern Europe, the cold and the hunger of these years. In subsequent years, the child grew to be an adult who showed all the symptoms of deprivation which we find in those who never experience positive mothering. She showed a definite lack in strong inner images and could not establish a warm and satisfying relationship with a partner, but constantly felt a gnawing sense of inner solitude. She also, as she explained it to me later, needed to be able to feel that she could leave relationships again and again. Otherwise she felt trapped.

THE SYMPTOMS OF SOLITUDE
∽

But what are the symptoms of solitude and what lies behind them? The person concerned feels alone in an unempathic world. This is actually a projection of an intrapsychic situation. One sees and feels something which is an inherent part of oneself as coming from the world outside. Within the individual's own psyche there is a serious lack of empathy; the person actually lacks understanding toward him- or herself. Psychology thinks that this lack develops in the following way. A very young child really does experience this lack in the outer world; the child can certainly in no way understand or formulate it, but suffers nonetheless. Things one cannot understand, especially painful ones, one tends to repress.

We can also say that we tend to withdraw our attention from experiences that are too painful; their connection with consciousness or awareness gets lost: we cannot concentrate our attention on them; therefore, we cannot understand them. We pretend that this is not happening: all of this belongs to the complex psychic activity called repression. Another aspect of repression involves the fact that, with time, we lose contact, not only with the memory of the painful experience, but also with that part of ourselves that was subjected to the experience. The emotional tie to this "experiencer" is dropped. Another explanatory model says that an empathic tie to ourselves never develops in the first place, for it has no model for development: we have not been exposed to the paradigmatic experience of a consistently caring person. Therefore, we do not know how to behave in such a way toward ourselves. No positive, reliable inner image can be internalized, because none has ever been developed: there was no opportunity to experience such a positive relationship.

On the background of such an emotional wasteland a generalized tone of depression develops. Hopelessness and sadness rule, a sense of the meaninglessness of life and the world prevails. Our own life seems terribly empty. Necessarily, relationships in the outer world become difficult. And, vice-versa, we tend to retreat from the outer world, all the while regretting the lack of contact, bemoaning our solitude. The only thing that remains is a need to prove ourselves through achievement. And this achievement-orientation forces us to try to perform inhuman feats, to become strong and capable, to fight, and not to allow weakness and sadness to exist. We come to neglect our own feelings and needs. The weak sense of self-esteem, which is part and parcel of the problem, can actually be understood as a weak sense of self, or a deficiency in the connection to our own deeper, inner being. But for the person concerned, the only tangible, more or less concrete feeling is a sense of being abandoned: we feel alone and desperate in this truly unbearable aloneness. We feel rejected and in suffering from rejection, we isolate ourselves further still.

THE DYNAMICS OF SOLITUDE
ᴄᴏ·

Suffering from solitude plays a central role in Grimms' fairy tale *Hansel and Gretel*. Here we can discover more about the dynamics of the problem. The tale shows possible developmental processes, steps leading through and eventually out of solitude and on to a deeper capacity for relationship with oneself and with the world. In considering the fairy tale we shall be interpreting it as the inner-psychic experience of a composite individual, Hansel-Gretel.

At the beginning of the tale, Hansel and Gretel are shown living in a severely deficient, we can even say, depressed state: there is little to eat; there is little human warmth. Their father, a poor woodsman, can no longer provide for the family. Their mother seems to have no feeling for her own children: she suggests that the father abandon them in the woods so that at least she and her husband can survive. Although the father is not happy with this solution, he consents. This is the trigger for the developmental process which is to follow. It is a process full of pain.

What does the initial situation actually mean? We have here a weak father. He can neither provide for his family nor can he stand up for himself or for his children. He obeys his wife who actually, therefore, gets pushed into the role of leader. She has the pants on, as we say, and he has the more feminine, or perhaps, the more passive role. But what does this mean for the children? In one word: abandonment. They have neither a father who can support and guide them, nor a mother who can love and care for them. In this way, they are really very poor. They lack support in both the maternal and the paternal domains. This can be interpreted in two ways. Either the relationships are really deficient because of an incapacity of the parents—a deficiency in their personal psychology: the mother is cut off from her feelings, the father cut off from his strength. Or, both parents seem ineffectual because the time has come when the children must leave the haven of their home and venture out into the world on their own. Both interpretations refer to a blockage in the developmental process. The latter corresponds more to the normal course of things: all parents have to become ineffectual at some time so that the children can go on with their lives themselves. In either case the children must come to leave their childhood positions for more mature ones. And it seems that, as in real life, here, too, they must be exposed to the experience of solitude in the sense of being alone, on their own, in order to reach new levels of relating and development. They must give up the security of home to try out their own wings.

The polyvalence of being thrown out of the nest—of being abandoned and exposed to solitude and insecurity—is well reflected in the image of being abandoned in the woods. For, on

the one hand, this means being exposed to true physical danger—
of starvation and of being eaten by wild animals—lacking care,
empathy, support, or nourishment: here there is no light nor joy
in life, only a dreadful sense of being lost and rejected. But, on the
other hand, this means being exposed to the possibility of making
encounters, discoveries: it is right here that things that are lurking
in the deeps can be encountered. It is here that Hansel and Gretel
actually meet up with those figures, fantasies, and feelings which
they need to realize in order to grow up. In psychological terms,
we would say that this forced disorientation is actually a moment
of re-orientation, allowing Hansel and Gretel to encounter as yet
unconscious aspects of themselves. This means that transformation becomes possible. And so, getting lost in the forest provokes
the children's encounter with their psychic depths, an encounter
which would not have been possible had they remained in their
parental home.

They way in which the children get lost is significant. The
first time they are led into the woods to starve, Hansel and Gretel
find their way back home. Hansel has overheard the plan and col-
lects pebbles with which he then strews the way. They follow the
pebbles back to the house. Actually this must be seen as a regressive step, back to the initially unsatisfying situation. The second
attempt to find the way back, this time with bread crumbs strewn
along the way, is unsuccessful, for birds have eaten the bread
crumbs. Hansel, who must have lived on the edge of the forest all
his life, should have known nature well enough to realize that this
would happen. This misjudging of nature shows that Hansel is
lacking in a sense of reality. This may have to do with his imma-
turity: young people often have not as yet had sufficient experience
of reality to be able to judge it realistically. This deficiency will
continue to cause Hansel and Gretel serious problems. It is this
domain of their experience which must drastically improve in
order for them to mature.

But what do the children meet in the forest? First of all, they
see the white bird which leads them to the witch's house. The bird,
as birds in general, has to do with the sphere of the air, with the
flighty, with the domain of the intellect, in contrast to the realm of

earth and matter. The fact that it is a white bird underlines this idea, for white is a color that generally represents purity and absolute values—here perhaps it is the realm of the intellectual or the spiritual, but in the sense of the ethereal. Concrete material reality, knowledge of the way things are in this world, entails a good relationship to earth and matter; whereas, flight to airier realms indicates a fascination with spirituality; it is not infrequently an escape from the difficulties involved in real life. Teenagers usually get involved in idealistic visions during the process of finding the appropriate distance from the paternal world and its values. New ideas and visions of the world lead them away from the family into a more independent realm. In our day and age this often unfortunately entails a refusal of the material in the form of the body and leads to serious anorectic problems. In refusing themselves sustenance they are acting out their need to put distance between themselves and the mother, the family, the womb, and haven of home. As we shall see in our case example following, such tendencies are often found in people whose experiences of mothering have been unsatisfactory. Living in the airy realm of ideas and visions is meant to compensate for the poor perception of and relationship to material reality, and in a certain way it does, for had Hansel and Gretel not followed the white bird, they never would have met the witch, and would never have had this developmental possibility.

But, where does the white bird lead the children? To the witch's house, the house made of all kinds of nice, sweet things to eat. The children pounce upon it and eat of its sweets without the slightest suspicion. And when they get into the snowy white sheets at night, they think that they are in heaven. On first glance, we can imagine that such a reaction is quite natural for children who have been so starved for food and for love and comfort. But, one does wonder at the naiveté with which they accept the goodness that seems to be laid out especially for them—in the middle of the forest. Again we are reminded of Hansel's naively strewing the bread crumbs. These children obviously have a serious defect in their relationship to material reality.

The witch, who has prepared all these temptations for the children, and then holds them captive, intending to eat them, symbolizes the basic problem. We can imagine her as a person who offers a child a lot of nice things in order to hold its affections, in order to bind the child to him or her. Her promise is, "You will never be alone again." Behind it is the threat, "But you will never again be free." The witch holds the child captive and wants to eat it, because in buying its affection in this way, the witch prevents the child's free and natural development. Behind the niceness, the intent is evil. Such a relationship is binding for the child who cannot easily sever the bonds of attachment.

The witch also has other specifically witch-like qualities: she cannot see well, but she can understand and speak the language of the animals in the forest where she lives. What does this mean? Not being able to see well, the witch cannot differentiate with an act of consciousness, but she feels her way along. She lives in what we call a *participation* with nature, a symbiotic relationship where there are no boundaries. It is actually this type of relationship problem which is central in Hansel and Gretel's case. Emotionally deprived as the children are, they long for a heaven-like state, one in which no conflict or differentiation exists. But the witch who offers so much containment and holding, in such an extreme way, is too much. She represents their symbiotic desires, which flourish in the unconscious, perhaps because they have been insufficiently satisfied during the appropriate phase of development. She represents their naive expectation of goodness and truth in the world, their hopes for complete dependency, for a paradisical state in which there is neither conflict nor strife. But such a state is inimical to any development.

But the encounter with the symbiotic domain of the witch enables the children to begin to see things as they are. This may be the only way that they can really get to know their own symbiotic desires, and the dangers that are inherent in them—being eaten up, ingurgitated by the overpowering maternal figure, being destroyed. Care and dependency are what the children crave; but, as they learn, it is a completely consuming state, absolutely inimical to life. The very intensity of the experience is probably what ultimately helps them to realize the dangers of living out these wishes. The children learn to develop their own trickiness and to outdo the witch. They get her to think that Hansel holds out his finger to be tested for just the right plumpness; instead he holds out a chicken bone. Gretel finally pushes the witch into the oven. On these occasions, it is Gretel who has the foresight and the good ideas. She is evidently learning that the witch has ulterior motives and that she, too, can trick her.

Finally, the tale tells how the children, having pushed the witch into the oven, free themselves and take her riches. On the way back home, they are carried by a duck who takes them across the water, but one after the other. They have become so aware of the reality of nature that Gretel realizes the duck cannot possibly carry both of them at the same time. What a great developmental step the children have taken! The newly acquired realism in their view of reality is indicated in Gretel's appreciation of the reality of nature: they are too heavy for the little duck. This knowledge of the boundaries of nature shows that the children are no longer caught in their symbiotic wishes of *participation*—their hungry need of a melting with the maternal. And their return home shows that they have conquered the negative mother, for she is dead and they and their father can enjoy the riches they have taken from the witch. The negative mother witch has been destroyed and they can profit from their experience with this utterly negative and ensnaring figure. She brings riches, for she has been seen and recognized for her negative qualities. They have become capable of seeing and judging material reality. Therefore, they can go home and establish a relationship with their father, who, now alone, without the cruel mother, can rejoice in his children. The fact that the cruel mother is gone probably has to do with the witch. This ensnaring aspect of the mother archetype is depotentiated when the unempathic mother is gone.

Hansel and Gretel shows us further aspects of the suffering from solitude. We see here how the lack of a positive experience of mothering, and consequently a lack of a reliable and positive inner image of a mother, determines the way the children perceive and experience life. They are completely out of touch with material reality and harbor naive expectations about it; they cherish unrealistic and dangerous symbiotic fantasies. Thus, they can become prisoners of the negative mother who intends to devour them. Their lack of a rounded-out experience of mothering leaves the children at a loss to deal with the reality of the negative mother. The lack of empathy which characterized their initial situation drags them down into the depressive clutches of the negative mother. But Gretel manages to trick the witch and the children escape from this emotionally crippling situation.

HANSEL AND GRETEL IN REAL LIFE

∾

What can this fairy tale situation look like in real life? A case example from my analytical practice will serve as an illustration and concretization of the pattern described above: here the sense of loneliness we have been describing, the way it can affect a person's life, and what it can take to grow out of it, will become clearer. The young woman who came to see me was dressed in a long black coat, her shoulders hunched over, her air quite detached. In this first hour, as in many of the hours to come, she radiated a very impressive aura of mistrust. Her complaint was that she had trouble with her oral presentations at university as well as in her contacts with fellow students. She thought they did not like her and was very embarrassed when she had to speak before them. During this first hour she mentioned briefly, and with no show of emotion, that she had been brought up in an orphanage.

As I was to discover in the hours to come, Jane, as I would like to call her, was very intellectually oriented: she reflected a lot on a philosophical level about love and life. In fact, she was studying philosophy. This bent had already been part of her very early life. In the orphanage, for example, she would fantasize about being a prophetess, standing on top of a lofty tower and making grand pronouncements to the world below her. This brief sketch reminds us of one of the elements which we have seen in *Hansel and Gretel*: the retreat into a world of ideas when the basis for a sound attachment to a more material realm is defective. This is quite the stereotype of the teenager who comes to reject the warmth of the family nest and prefers to fly off, in his or her imagination at least, into a more worthy, more intellectual world of ideas.

Jane was robbed of her mother very early on in her life: she was put in the orphanage around age 2. But being separated from her mother was only one aspect of the maternal nest taken from her. Gone with the mother was not only the security of a caring or nourishing parent, but also the home environment which naturally grants a child a sense of security: home always has a special importance to children. It is like an extension of mother and can itself, like the child's own room and his or her toys, in itself provide comfort and security. The stable physical environment, the material world associated with mother and the comforting regular rituals of daily life at home, is a kind of transitional object. That is, the reality of this material world calls up associations within the child of the mother, perhaps even of the initial maternal womb. It provides a transition, a bridge to mother and comfort. When the one is sufficiently present and sensible, then the other is guaranteed. On the contrary, when this is not the case, instability, insecurity, and even fear can be evoked in the child. We saw this in the preceding example of the young refugee in war-torn Europe of the post war years. But Jane's experience was brought to an abrupt end. How did she deal with it? She repressed the awareness of her early abandonment, as we see in her unemotional statement about being brought up in an orphanage. But, already at a very young age, Jane learned to turn off her emotions; not only were they too painful for her, they were too painful for her milieu. Whenever her mother or father brought her back to the orphanage after a weekend visiting with one of the grandmothers, she was told not to cry. One can well imagine how difficult it must have been for both the parents and the child when she did cry and plead not to be taken back to the orphanage. And so, it is quite understandable that Jane obediently learned to avoid the world of her sorrow and pain. Instead, she fled into a world of ideas and spirituality. Here she could reflect on higher things and revel in fantasies of grandeur (like that of being a prophetess). Here no one could reach her and tell her what to do. No one could destroy the frail sense of self-esteem which she built for herself. Jane, like most of those suffering from solitude, lived in a Cinderella-like fantasy world with expectations of being discovered by the prince and eventually becoming the queen. But we shall be getting into this aspect of the experience of solitude in the next chapter.

The lack of empathy Jane necessarily felt at being abandoned by Mother, and at living in a foreign milieu that was not home, became a generalized feeling. It was the world which was not empathic. This is quite obvious when we think back to the transition which seems to exist in the child's mind between mother and mother's world. Of foremost importance, however, is that the lack of empathy she experienced outside became an inner mode of relating, or rather of not relating, to herself. Jane could not have positive, warm, and supportive feelings toward herself. Once again, when we think back to the small child, all of this becomes comprehensible. A child is not strong or independent enough to develop and sustain such feelings without having a firm anchor for them in the outer world. In other words, the inner image of mother and mothering must be experienced frequently, and intensely enough to be ingrained in the child's being. Obviously with mother and the mothering environment gone at age 2, Jane was at a loss to carry on these all-important feelings and functions for herself.

She became suspicious of the world, while at the same time harboring secret and grandiose fantasies about her own worth, and similarly unrealistic wishes for relationships. She needed them to be utterly harmonious and caring, even symbiotic. Naturally she was disappointed again and again. And so, she was not able to meet others with openness and confidence. She suspected, unconsciously, that the others would react like her mother and reject her, leaving her once again alone and lonely, once she had allowed herself to open up in a relationship. Such an attitude necessarily isolated Jane even further. Tragically, her weak sense of self-esteem could not be corrected or bolstered by any positive experiences, for she could not be open to the latter. Her expectations of disappointment determined her actual experiences of disappointment. And then, in turn, retreating from the world, she retreated from herself, too.

The naive expectations toward the world were the very destructive other side of the matter. Cherishing naive hopes of how people should treat her, she was naturally always disappointed. The world was made of gingerbread in her hopes and fantasies. Whenever it was bitter and not sweet, she became more lonely and depressed. Jane was not able to look at people, the world, life situations and see them for what they really were. And so, she could not make realistic judgments about how people were, or how they reacted toward her. She always felt slighted, because her expectations were much too high. Jane was caught in the trap of the negative mother, utterly alone and abandoned, suffering greatly from solitude, but basically, from solitude from her own being, from her self or her Self.

In the course of therapy, however, Jane was able to make some important experiences. First of all, and of prime importance, she needed to find in me, her therapist, someone who was open to her and ready to listen and empathize with her. I had to be there to listen to her distress, her disappointment, and her loneliness. That also meant, in Jane's case specifically, being there, available. It meant offering her my private number in case of an emergency. And, although she very rarely made use of this privilege, it was important for her to know that she had it. It gave her a sense of security: she could feel held by a person whom she had decided to confide in.

On the basis of this trust, which, I must add, was extremely difficult to establish, Jane slowly became capable of opening up—to herself, to me, and to the world. The pain of her early, much too early experience of abandonment and subsequent solitude became evident to her and needed a long period of adjustment, that it was possible, that it had been. And it needed to be digested. It had been a traumatic experience and had been followed by the long-lasting pain of life in the orphanage. As she began to develop a sense of the child who she had been and its pain, Jane was developing a sense of empathy for herself as a human being, then and now. This is the all-important key to psychotherapeutic processes. It made Jane capable of making positive experiences in the realm of emotions. She could give up some of her skepticism toward people, and could abandon some of the unrealistic fantasy images of the all-embracing mother (who is also the flip side of the witch or the ensnaring mother) and became capable of seeing and observing the real world for what it was. It was no longer necessarily so evil, for she could see it, and was not always only seeing the extension of her negative mother experience. A strong inner image of positive mothering had to be provided by the therapist. Slowly this image could be internalized. The space accorded to the all-embracing and the devouring mother pole was taken up by this more positive but more realistic image. At the end of the therapy, Jane was also able to realize when she was too heavy for the little duck.

As we see here, a concomitant aspect of these new experiences is a sense of not being so alone, lonely, isolated, rejected by a cruel world. The more realistic reliable mother figure (which is internalized) aids in this process. Another aspect of mother is, however, not negligible: the archetypal aspect, as it can be experienced in the outer world. Mother nature became a new maternal lap for Jane. She became open to her as she spontaneously sought contact with the woods. Nature and the woods gave Jane a sense of belonging to a greater world in which all are accepted and held. This was a comforting thought and feeling for Jane. On the same level, Jane became more and more aware of her own body. She began to learn to sense when she did not feel well and to learn to care for herself in such moments. This may seem banal, but when one has worked intimately with people who have a negative or non-existing contact with their bodies, with their whole material world, then the renewal which a new sense of rapport can mean is quite immediately apparent. It is quite a leap from a person who goes out in bad weather with ballerina slippers to someone who feels a cold coming on, dresses accordingly, makes him- or herself a cup of hot tea, and goes to bed early. Jane also began to be able to become a good mother for herself. The physical level of this expression complements and accompanies the emotional level.

At the end of our lengthy therapy (eight years), Jane had become a person who knew and appreciated the pain of her early abandonment and realized how it had consequently affected her capacity for relationships, how it had made her skeptical of people and also expectant of a naive fulfillment of denied symbiotic wishes. She no longer suffered from the solitude of her early youth. Inwardly, she was no longer alone: she carried her own inner child, as many dream images toward the end of therapy quite explicitly said. She also had a circle of friends whom she liked, and a boyfriend whom she ultimately married. She completed her philosophy studies at university and went on to become a kindergarten teacher. Having come to be able to relate to herself, she became capable of relating to others. She no longer automatically projected this terribly negative inner image onto the world, but could see and judge those around her realistically. This, of course, also made her more capable of entering into normal relationships. Jane remained a person whose gifts were intellectual—they were well trained throughout all of those years. But her intellect was no longer the only function she could rely on.

PSYCHOTHERAPY

～

When people seek out a psychotherapist, it is inevitably at a time of need, when the need is felt for clarity, order, and solid support in a time of extreme duress. People today are generally too independently-minded to be able to ask for help readily or easily. So, they must feel that there is something quite seriously wrong to make them take such a step. A lack of appropriately empathic inner images (which could give the necessary security and confidence to get through the crisis) leads them to seek such a figure in the outside world—in the form of a psychotherapist. From this point of view, we can say that people who seek psychotherapy feel in some important way alone and needy and suffer accordingly. Whether we think here of those going through separation from a loved one—through death, divorce or, even moving out—or whether we think of those dealing with pangs of anxiety that come up as from nowhere, those who feel insecure, who have bouts of fainting or other disturbing psychosomatic problems, all are actually in need of a secure relationship to supportive inner images. People may feel the need to be related to other people—or not. The bottom line of their need, although this is seldom clear to them—is the need to feel related to themselves and to their own supportive inner forces.

The very worst aspect of solitude is the solitude from our own inner self. This is the situation we have seen in Hansel and Gretel, who go through a developmental process in order to retrieve their sense of self, or who they are. In therapy, people go through similar processes, coming to realize their hunger, their abandonment, their naive expectations, and coming to see reality for what it is. They must come to meet their own inner witch, who invariably has seduced them and held them in her ban. And they can emerge from this inner odyssey with riches untold that make them capable of pursuing a fulfilled life as adults grounded in themselves and capable of forming relationships. They are no longer alone, for the image of the therapist, internalized during the therapeutic process, has become their own; it accompanies them and serves as a support and guide for the future. The final chapter of this book is devoted to a detailed look at such processes.

FEAR OF SOLITUDE AS THE PRESENTING PROBLEM

∾·

I would like to go on to speak of another case that shows the really terrible fears which the threat of solitude can unleash in a seemingly mature adult. This is the story of a woman, age 40, whose children were just about ready to leave home. But Mrs. Z came to see me because of what seemed to her inexplicable bouts of panic. Having come up out of the blue, they threw her into terrible agitation, tinged with feelings of her inferiority. It took quite some time for Mrs. Z to realize that she actually did have anxieties about something quite real—being alone, without her children and faced with a life with her husband. He was a loner, had always been so, and provided her with little or no company, or emotional support, or comfort. She had always been a self-sufficient type; she called herself a "wash and wear" woman— easy to be with, not demanding, readily satisfied. Actually, analytically speaking, Mrs. Z was not afraid of being alone; she *was* alone and was feeling it for the first time. It was a deep inner solitude: a retreat had taken place very early on in her life, a retreat from the person with wishes, hopes, desires, and needs of love, warmth, and comfort from her surroundings. As a little girl, she had tried very hard to live up to her parents' expectations. She had somehow got the message that she had to, otherwise she would be very alone and lonely. Affection, she felt, depended on performance.

But the inner psychic consequences for such an adaptation are grave: Mrs. Z's own inner images were only supporting and positive when she continued, as an adult, to perform well, with the expected excellence. As a mother, she had had little difficulty fulfilling her expectation of herself: the children and the house were kept clean and proper; the children turned out quite well and became serious professional people. But now came the greatest challenge. How was she to perform well beside a withdrawn partner who demanded little of her, with little to do in the home, no one to take care of? At this point in her life Mrs. Z was at a loss to imagine how she could go on. Her early needs for affection, understanding, for a close, emotionally satisfying relationship she had smothered early on. As one approaches the middle of life, such needs can surface again. And so we see how older men seek beautiful, young mistresses and their wives turn to them for the warm and loving relationship they never had before.

Mrs. Z and I had to go back together to retrieve an abandoned and needy little girl. We had to find her and persuade her to open up and talk of all that she had experienced—the pleasures, but also the sorrows at not being held and comforted when she so needed it. We had to try to establish an empathic contact with her. Often, as we know, a child can seem so self-sufficient that one hesitates to treat it like a child. We can only hope that the child's malleable psyche is capable of allowing the regressive longings to be and to be expressed. So we find children who run off as wild adventurers during the day and crawl into their parents' beds at night.

This is the kind of compensation necessary for the overly self-sufficient child. Problems arise when these compensatory gestures are not allowed to be, are misunderstood, or are not taken seriously. If the child is healthy, which is more often the case than not, then the compensatory gesture will arise. It is then the parents' job to hear and pay attention to it. This task was more difficult than one might imagine, for Mrs. Z had become a very demanding parent toward herself. She was harsh in her judgments of herself and not ready to listen to her own needs. Her expectations for achievement and perfection were as strong, perhaps they were even stronger, than her parents expectations had been.

This is obviously the domain of the wicked witch: she seems too offer goodies as a reward for good performance, but she actually holds fast in an unconscious realm where abandonment is the only way of being. The wishes in this unconscious realm are of symbiosis: Hansel and Gretel want to be eaten together. It is this wish that inevitably holds one prisoner. If I perform well, then I will be loved. But such calculations are false. More expectations come: everything becomes entirely unrealistic. One cannot carry all this weight of responsibility. And this is what Mrs. Z and Hansel and Gretel had to come to realize.

Hansel and Gretel, and Mrs. Z and Jane may seem too extreme examples when one is talking about suffering from solitude in "normal" people today. The tendency is, however, identical in all, no matter how far or how deep the problem goes. I would even go as far as saying that everyone suffers from solitude at some point in his or her life: the basic phenomenology of the experience is the same for all. We feel a lack in the domain of relationships, an empathic contact is missing, and our sense of being someone feels endangered because of this lack, i.e., our sense of self-esteem becomes unstable. Determinant to the degree of despair such feeling evoke in us is most likely the strength of the positive inner images. The more reliable they are, the less despairing we need be that meaningful relationships are lacking for a certain time.

Solitude and suffering from it, as I said in the initial pages of this chapter, must be part of what it means to be human. I mentioned attachment behavior as the reason. We can also say that love leads us to the peak of suffering from solitude. I would further like

to suggest that development is only possible when a certain proportion of solitude is feasible: maturation processes need not only relationships, they also need periods of solitude, even isolation from
others—incubation. The question is how much of each and when.

DEPRESSION, INTENSE AND SHAMEFUL EXPERIENCES

∽·

There is hardly another psychic
illness which is more closely identified with solitude than depression.
Early images, for example, Albrecht Dürer's *Melencolia*, well attest
to this fact. People who are alone are often depressed; the depressed
person feels alone and abandoned, all the while tending to isolate
himself. Aristotle noticed this seeming paradox already in the fourth
century B.J.C.E.[11] One excellent example of this paradox is the example of Bellerophon: we shall be examining it in detail in the final
chapter. Suffice to say now that it is a well-known fact that depressive people feel abandoned, and, at the same time, seclude themselves from the world.[12] Perhaps our example from *Hansel and
Gretel* will help to explain this phenomenon. Hansel and Gretel's
venture into the forest can be seen as a deep depression. It is a time
of introversion in which images from the unconscious can be constellated. The wicked witch can then appear and one can, if the light
of consciousness falls upon the witch, realize that she is a devouring,
negative figure. But the wishes are definitely of being spoiled.
Feelings of low self-esteem combine with unrealistic wishes for
dependency. Being alone is being alone with the evil witch, who
holds one in her grasp. It is not so easy to see the witch and what
she offers for what they are—as unrealistic symbiotic wishes. This is
the wish for dependency and the helplessness that it leads to. The
vicious circle is difficult to break because of the lack of initiative

---

11. Aristoteles, "Das Problem XXX" in Erwin Panofsky, Raymond Klibansky, and
Fritz Saxl, *Saturn und Melencolie* (Frankfurt: Suhrkamp, 1990).
12. Aaron T. Beck, *Depression: Causes & Treatment* (Philadelphia: University of
Pennsylvania Press, 1972). See chapter 2, "Symptomology of Depression."

which is characteristic of depression. The basic lack here is that of a positive inner figure who can hold and support one in times of need.

But depressive people are not the only ones who suffer from solitude because of their state of mind. Any intense psychic experience can lead one into the depths of solitude. One feels alone and not understood, isolated, singled out because of the uniquely terrible or terrifying experience one is in. Deep fears, terrible jealousy, excruciating embarrassment, despair, anger—almost any feeling of a negative quality and of a certain magnitude can lead one to feel isolated, but also to retreat in isolation. The experience is so all involving that one feels that no one else can understand it, can sympathize, or empathize with it. A further element is shame. The more one is ashamed of these feelings, i.e., the less one can admit that one has them and it is valid to have them, the greater the tendency to isolation. Actually, it must be evident for the reader here that all of this is projection. It is the empathic inner figure who is missing, no one is there who understands and empathizes, but this no one is on the inside. There is no inner figure who can listen to and try to understand the pain and the difficulty of the situation. The inner ear is deaf to one's own suffering. The notion that the world does not understand, that nobody understands, even that everybody is ridiculing one, is a pure projection: one is not empathic to oneself. The truth of this idea reveals itself in psychotherapy, when the analyst becomes the first person to lend an ear to the sufferer. With time the patient must come to develop a similar understanding attitude to himself or herself, otherwise no therapeutic process takes place.

In this respect, shame is an important phenomenon.[13] Shame isolates. It is both a stumbling block and a first step toward realization and cure. Being ashamed of one's emotions or deeds, one's body or mind shows that which is shameful is important. It is so

---

13. Mario Jacoby, *Scham-Angst und Selbstwertgefühl: ihre Bedeutung in der Psychotherapie* (Olten: Walter Verlag, 1991). This contemporary Jungian analyst is especially interested in Kohut's self-psychology in relation to Jungian psychology. Readers may want to explore: *Individuation & Narcissism: The Psychology of Self in Jung & Kohut* (London: Routledge, 1990); and *The Longing for Paradise: Psychological Perspectives in an Archetype*, translated by Myron Gubitz (Boston: Sigo, 1985).

Figure 5. "Melencolia I," by Albrecht Dürer, 1514. Woodcut.

important that it takes up a lot of space, emotion, and energy. It becomes a question of prime importance. If, however, the shame can be so overcome that one can speak of the experience (the word, the deed, the feeling), then its importance can be realized. The whole event of recounting the shameful thing is valuable: being able to confide in someone changes a person on a very deep level. It means also that a certain extent of acceptance has been found: the unpronounceable can be pronounced, and so certain aspects of oneself, which one tried to exclude, start to become isolated. Certain aspects of oneself from which one tended to withdraw, and which led to isolation from oneself and others, can be integrated.

Isolation from others can be sensed as such, but can be mainly and initially an internal, intrapsychic affair. One is alone, solitary, isolated when one is abandoning aspects of oneself. One feels, however, that it is the world which is doing the abandoning. The wicked witch is really inside, not outside. And she can only be vanquished when she is kept in place, when she is put in her place, i.e., seen as an inner figure and not an outer manifestation, something for which the world outside alone is responsible. This type of solution requires initiative, energy, and hope. Despair and fatalism are major enemies and immense stumbling blocks in any effort to escape from solitude. One must be able to see the situation for what it is, to realize one's projections onto the world, the projection of the abandoning mother and the projected expectations of the spoiling and ensnaring mother. The symbiotic wishes and fantasies for help, dependency, and abundant presents or favors from the world around are just as damaging and ensnaring as the fantasies of not being understood. But it is easier for most people to put themselves in the victim position than in charge of their own fate.

SOLITUDE AND LOVE
ᠵ

Solitude plays an important role in love, but as this is not a book about relationships, we can dwell on this interesting topic but briefly. Lovers suffer from separation from each other, often they wish for a shared solitude, to go off to be alone together. Not infrequently, a love relationship does not satisfy one of the partner's needs for togetherness, and he or she suffers from being together but feeling very alone.

Separation is accordingly an important theme in love. We know that when we fall in love the presence of the other becomes an all important ingredient for our happiness. The more we know each other, the more "absence makes the heart grow fonder." In the initial pages of this chapter, we spoke of death and banishment as archetypal situations in which humanity experiences the negative side of solitude. The basic problem can be seen as separation from a loved one. Poems and literary works have often been devoted to this theme, so well known to lovers throughout the world at all times. A 14th-century poem by Shota Rustaveli called *The Lord of the Panther Skin* is a very early example of such suffering. The poem is preceded by a prologue in which the author says, "when the loved one is far away, The lover's breath becomes a sigh." He even goes as far as to distinguish true love from a flirt according to the depth of the pain one feels at the separation:

> The lover must be constant and free from all stain and adultery; when parted from his lady he should for ever be sighing; his heart must yearn for one and one only, though she be cruel and unkind. . . . This one today, that other tomorrow; parting without a pang—this is not worthy of the name of love!

This early Georgian author states, as many a lover today would, when he is far away, he melts in nostalgia, eating up his heart "in the embers of the flame."[14] In this very intense and somewhat antiquated dramatic poetic language, Rustaveli is expressing the same type of feelings as Shakespeare did in *Romeo and Juliet* or others have in films like *West Side Story*.

People in love often wish to be apart from the rest of the world and just be together. They can fantasize about fleeing from society, even about a common suicide which will set them apart

14. Shota Rustaveli, *The Lord of the Panther Skin*, translated by R. H. Stevenson (Albany: State University of New York Press, 1977), p. 5, 6.

from the world and from the banality of life in the world. Being in love often means feeling such special feelings that the very specialness of the experience must be held as long as possible. The 19th-century French symbolist poet Villiers de l'Isle Adam describes this type of situation very impressively in his play *Axel*. It is not the danger of the surrounding world that the lovers flee in fantasies about a common suicide (*Romeo and Juliet*). Rather, they do not want their love to be soiled by the banality of day-to-day existence: they are desperate to retain the specialness of their feeling state by perpetuating it through death. But here we are in the presence of the search for solitude, actually the subject of our following chapter.

There are also other aspects in the question of the role solitude plays in love. Although love seems to promise the hope of being redeemed from solitude, there is necessarily a phase of disenchantment, when one realizes that this promise can never actually be fulfilled by another human being. The disappointment which arises can lead a person to feel alone and lost forever. Deep depression often ensues, or there is a search for a new partner who can perhaps better fulfill these desires. The pain of being together but feeling apart can be much more painful than lacking a love relationship. Pablo Neruda speaks for us in his poem, "Leaning into the Afternoons."

> *Leaning into the afternoons I cast my sad nets*
> *towards your oceanic eyes.*
>
> *There in the highest blaze my solitude lengthens and flames,*
> *its arms turning like a drowning man's.*
>
> *I send out red signals across your absent eyes*
> *that wave like the sea or the beach by a lighthouse.*
>
> *You keep only darkness, my distant female,*
> *from your regard sometimes the coast of dread emerges.*
>
> *Leaning into the afternoons I fling my sad nets*
> *to that sea that is thrashed by your oceanic eyes.*

*The birds of night peck at the first stars
that flash like my soul when I love you.*

*The night gallops on its shadowy mare
shedding blue tassels over the land.*[15]

CONCLUSION
❧

In conclusion to this chapter about suffering from solitude, it is most important to emphasize the main underlying psychological problem—lack of the appropriate inner figures. People who suffer inordinately from solitude seem to be lacking positive (i.e., supportive) inner structures or figures to which they feel related in an intimate way; they cannot rely on the company of these figures. But such a lack must be understood on a collective as well as on a personal level. Many people have not had good experiences in this domain, but the problem has to do with our day and age. Support can potentially come from many sources, but the modern predilection for the nuclear family necessarily precludes the reliability of a support system from a wide network of extended family relationships. And what else is there? What about the community? The most recent developments, migratory waves of politically and economically depressed people, and homeless hordes in big cities shape the new face of society—a motley group of people jumbled together with insufficiently supportive and nurturing value systems, with little in the way of shared values at all. Religion used to provide a support, god figures who held and comforted their people, providing them with security in uncertain political and physical situations, for example in the turbulent times of the

15. "Leaning into the Afternoons," in Pablo Neruda, *Selected Poems*, edited by Nathaniel Tarn, translated by Anthony Kerrigan, W. S. Merwin, Alaistar Reid, and Nathaniel Tarn (London: Jonathan Cape, 1966), p. 21.

Middle Ages. Most religious and cultural values (support systems) have lost importance today. Contemporary people are certainly no longer held by a collective in a social and spiritual universe that provides meaning and strength for life. The little child Moses of the end of the 20th century no longer has a people, nor a God to whom he feels he belongs. His exile is from himself, his mother, his country of origin: this brings him, according to inexorable psychological laws, to live in an inner wasteland which he generally tends to project onto society. He is plagued with feelings of poor self-esteem, self-doubt, and a vacuum with nowhere to turn: all of this he attempts to alleviate by various means, from achievement and acquisition, to drugs and television. But actually the Moses of our age is subjected to a deep sense of inner solitude that cannot really be alleviated, for it is entrenched in his innermost self. When he senses that this is so, he can try to forget or perhaps to sleep, or to eke out an existence in the depressive depths of the forest. The hope is that he will eventually awaken and find the energy and initiative to be able to push the witch back into her own oven. Very frequently, however, contemporaries stay at the witch's house, eating her gingerbread and seeking distraction from the depression. The apparently good things here seem to offer satisfaction for the deep psychic hunger of the solitary. When the witch reaches out to eat him, he has neither the strength, nor the hope, nor the initiative to try to learn to deal with her, to put her in her place.

Before concluding this chapter, I must remind the reader of the importance of the other side of the question. We caught a brief glimpse of it in *Hansel and Gretel*. Painful though it is, the experience of solitude makes one human. It can be valuable, as the spiritually inclined have known for many generations. One can even go so far as to say that joys and temptations are involved in the pleasures people can draw from solitude. This is the subject of our next chapter.

CHAPTER TWO

The Search for Solitude

The Pleasures and Temptations of Solitude

*I*f it really is so that human beings have an archetypal need for community, for kinship, for a feeling of relatedness, how can we understand the fact that some people, instead of complaining of their suffering from solitude, declare their love of solitude and, furthermore, that most people speak of a need to be alone at least some of the time? The truth of the matter is actually that the cultivation of solitude knows a long tradition, with both sacred and profane manifestations. At the root of both is the same basic striving: a search for transcendence. They both also share the same basic temptation: that of fantasies of grandeur. The solitary search of the hermit saints, shamans, and religious leaders for communion with God is obvious. In their solitary retreat to nature Romantic poets, too, sought a deepened contact—this time to a certain elevated, poetic frame of mind and being. People today also speak of their search for a connection to another area of sensitivity, one beyond the normal state of being. Furthermore, many contemporaries seek in solitude to develop their own personal brand of individualism. Many people even choose to live alone (a widespread phenomenon that we have come to refer to as the Singles' Society). They speak of wanting to get away from feeling obligated to others, of needing rest and regeneration, of enjoying a heightened sense of pleasure, of the new and pleasantly different sensitive awareness which they can enjoy in solitary and quasi-meditative states. Often the declared need is the development of one's own personality; people attempt to find their own individualistic lifestyle, with a minimum of conformity to social pressures. But the bottom line and very unconscious goal of all of these searches for solitude—from the saints to the poets, to the individualists, is the search for something beyond the commonplace. I would say quite unequivocally, that this is a search for transcendence. For solitude, even today, is far from the commonplace living within a community.

The Bible tells us that God made Eve to be Adam's companion and helper, "for it is not good for man to be alone."[1] Accordingly, Jewish tradition considers an unmarried person only half a person. This idea is absolutely in line with Plato's image of the syzygy: man and woman were originally created as one whole being and were only separated when they became too powerful, too strong for the gods.[2] The idea of the couple seems to be a very basic, historically founded and perhaps even archetypal, image of being. A human being necessarily belongs together with another one: the couple is created in order to be together. In this way, an elementary building block for community is established, a certain stability of society is granted and the survival of humanity is guaranteed.

Furthermore, according to the Chassidic masters, only God is truly alone, and He is to be pitied for this solitude.[3] This is because God is incomparable: he cannot possibly have a suitable partner. And so, in a certain way, whenever human beings seek solitude, they are imitating God and rejecting the human condition such as God conceived it for man (according to biblical history), and as people have tended to live it since at least this time. In their independent fashion of choosing their own style of life, people today are, in a certain way, choosing their own fate, deciding on their own, assuming the divine prerogative of how they want to live, and not allowing themselves to be dictated upon by society or by God. One could say that they are measuring themselves with, even per-

1. Genesis 2:18.
2. Plato, *The Symposium*. Walter Hamilton, trans. (New York: Viking/Penguin, 1952).
3. Elie Wiesel, "Keiner is allein wie Gott," [No One is as Alone as God] in Rudolf Walter, *Von der Kraft der sieben Einsamkeiten*, (Basel, Vienna, Freiburg: Herder, 1984), p. 112.

haps identifying with, God. Such a way of expressing it may seem too extreme; it only makes sense within a religious tradition of thought. Nevertheless, innumerable solitary figures of religious and profane tradition do bathe in divine images of themselves. But, to generalize, it is perhaps more fitting to say that whenever solitude is sought or cultivated, whenever people retreat to a solitary state, they are striving (perhaps unconsciously) for something beyond what is generally accepted, beyond the norm, for some kind of superiority. They are seeking excellence, a special, or unique position, comparable to that of God or other heroic figures.

The close association of solitude and superiority is found in the most varied of cultures throughout time. The solitary stone, like the diamond, is an especially precious gem, set apart in a special setting, alone; similarly, the hero is almost inevitably a lonely, or at least a lone, hero (classically, Hercules, Ulysses, and more recently the Lone Ranger, Superman, or Phillip Marlowe); a particularly daring, and, at the same time, necessarily a solitary figure; the artist, too, often lives in what has ironically been referred to as "splendid isolation." From this perspective, it is quite clear that a superior, even grandiose or inflated, image of oneself and one's capacities is a basic temptation involved in the search for solitude. The equation "seeking solitude = temptation of grandiosity" seems to find justification even in the stories of religious leaders of old: many religious leaders of great renown sought communion with their gods in meditative retreats far from society. They subsequently knew many temptations, one basic one being visions of their own superiority. This is true of Saint Anthony, as well as of Buddha and Jesus.

In this chapter, we shall be examining the various aspects of the cultivation of solitude; first of all, the tradition of the religious retreat in which, as in all forms of retreat, fantasies of grandiosity play an important role. The solitary position of healers, shamans, witches, and early doctors follows this same tradition. From there we shall go on to examine the vicissitudes of the solitary retreat throughout the ages in the Western world. Here we see that the religiously-motivated search for solitude is only one side of the question. A more profane search has been going on since the Renaissance: it has been undertaken in the name of "individualism." Contemporary idealization of individualism and independence can be seen as an attempt to retrieve or even to establish a sense of self. At a time when society does not provide the echo necessary to confirm one's identity, people tend to seek this sense of who they are in individualistic visions of independence and freedom. At the same time, a much less conscious need for the exact opposite is present among independence-minded contemporaries. Those clamoring for independence are generally deeply yearning for symbiotic situations, such as those which reign in the domain of Hansel and Gretel's witch. An adamant refusal and rejection of that which is deeply yearned for—denial and reversal—is a typical defense against the unconscious opposite which is always necessarily present in the psyche. Or, in Jung's words, when collective consciousness is so clearly dominated by one idea, it is, as in the individual psyche, necessarily one-sided. The other side is there, but in the unconscious; rejected, it is all the stronger.[4] A case example will help to illustrate this phenomenon.

People tend to retreat into solitude—often to the proverbial "lap of Mother Nature"—when their feelings have been hurt, when they feel misunderstood or rejected. Many famous people—from Petrarch to Rousseau and Thoreau—and, of course, many other, less famous ones belong to this "back to nature" movement. Withdrawal into the solitude of nature is necessary in the first place in order to help the person re-establish a sense of his or her identity and a sense of self-esteem. But all back to nature fantasies involve both symbiotic desires (of undifferentiated sameness, of unspoken understanding between human beings and nature, between the members of the group) and heroic pronouncements of self-righteous plans for the betterment of the human race. The bottom line, the seldom conscious motivation, behind this trend is rather a retreat prompted by the person's having been hurt, insulted, slighted, somehow wounded by the world. Mother Nature is then inevitably seen as consoling, all good, providing only goodness

---

4. This is a very basic Jungian concept. Readers not familiar with Jung's work can read more in C. G. Jung, *The Archetypes and the Collective Unconscious*, Collected Works, Vol. 9.I, R. F .C. Hull, trans., Bollingen Series XX (Princeton: Princeton University Press, 1959), §277.

and bounties. We shall go on from here to speak of Cinderella, a seemingly dejected young girl whose solitude, although it initially seems involuntary, actually turns out to be, in part, a matter of choice. The fairy tale shows how Cinderella's grandiose fantasies compensate for her dejection. But the process orientation of the tale shows us how a girl with a lowly sense of self-worth can become a princess, growing from a schizoid incapacity for relating (to her own feelings and to other people) to a mature woman capable of relationships. In order to do so she must own up to her self-isolating position and to her fantasies of grandeur. *Cinderella* offers us a paradigm for the recovery from a schizoid position.

The search for solitude knows innumerable variations. We all know that at certain times in normal, day-to-day life we just feel the need to be alone. What prods us is not dissimilar to what has prodded people throughout time: the search for something beyond us and our daily world, beyond our present state of being. This search can be a light but nonetheless necessary flight into a solitary pause—for the space of a few minutes, a few hours or a few days. It can also be an experience of greater import: it just feels necessary in order to re-establish an interrupted connection to oneself. There are also phases in life which seem to push us into more introverted states of being. The beginning of a new phase in development often requires a certain retreat, perhaps in order to keep the sense of self intact during the turmoil typical of all transformative processes. Illnesses during the course of which we are thrown back onto ourselves, in which a certain isolation from impulses from the outside world necessarily occurs, often announce a period of transition or transformation. And, on the other end of the spectrum, are those people who tend to seek retreat as a natural state of being: a certain relatively large proportion of solitude belongs to their natural sense of who they are. They may be introverted, schizoid, or what we call "loners." Societies seem to vary on the amount of solitude granted to the members without their being considered eccentric. Today we know the "Singles' Society," which is a modern variation on the "singles' scene." This is a much less eccentric version of the more radically isolated hippies or vagabonds of earlier years and of the geniuses or hermits of earlier cultures.

THE TRADITION OF RELIGIOUS RETREAT

◦·

Let us begin our examination of the search for solitude with the latter—that of the hermit. Christian church history abounds in examples of the religiously motivated search for solitude. From Jesus' own retreat into the desert, to the retreat of medieval monks and nuns to cloisters (cloister stems from the Latin word *claudere* and means "closed off"), the Christian church seems to have cultivated from the start a tradition of seeking transcendence in solitude. Teresa of Avila's account of the cloisters of her time[5] gives us a very everyday view of what seriously religious people like her must have been seeking in such seclusion. In her memoirs, she speaks of the "useless babbling" that went on in her cloisters. The nuns regularly had visits from family and friends and all chatted nicely—and, if we are to believe Teresa, continuously, of mundane things. Little time was left for the contemplation of more worthy religious matters. Apparently at this time—16th-century Spain—the isolation of the religious retreat was not very strictly observed. But the tendency to retreat, nevertheless, seems to be widespread throughout different periods and religions. Religiously-minded people of earlier times seem to have felt a need of rejecting the world of matter—of material concerns—in order to seek transcendence, often involving a more intimate contact with God. The sacrifice of joy in life and of social intercourse seems to have been the accustomed manner of attaining to a more spiritually elevated life. One very early model for such an attitude is Moses, who climbed to the top of mount Sinai alone, in order to converse with God and to receive the Ten Commandments. Symbolically, the mountain represents a place of solitude and elevation, a place of superiority, away from the common people and their cares and strife. At the foot of the mountain, the people worshipped the golden calf—an idol related to the more primitive, less culturally advanced, and, therefore, lowly cults of vegetation deities—and complained bitterly and impatiently that they needed water. Moses

---

5. "Das grosse Gespräch: Teresa von Avila 1515-1582" in Walter Nigg, Grosse Heilige, 1946 (Zurich: Diogenes, 1990).

had to go beyond all of this, to go above it, to transcend it, in order to come to a place where he could meet with God. This image is one of the basic ones behind the hermitage and the holy retreat, the *exercitiae* (religious retreats) which have become so closely identified with Christianity.

But images of solitude and retreat to more holy spheres of existence are common to most religions. We need merely recall here the story of Buddha, who left his life of luxury to seek enlightenment, wandering about like a hermit for six years until he finally sat down under a bodhi tree to await enlightenment. Forty-nine days passed before the man who sat down as Siddhartha Gautama could get up as Buddha—"the enlightened one."

What supposedly went on under the bodhi tree tells us more about the temptations lurking in solitude. It is the story of a legendary battle, of a temptation which takes place in the wilderness and, therefore, of a temptation quite specific to solitude. Mara, the tempter, attacks Buddha, first with a huge army, then with various natural catastrophes—rainstorms and rocks, coals and hot ashes, sand, mud, and darkness are all poured upon him. Then Mara proceeds to challenge Buddha's right to sit there: he questions his worthiness. But Buddha never gives in. No further details are provided on the trials, but I believe that they involve the temptation of grandiose self image fantasies which plague Buddha. First of all, there is the very obvious reference to the subject of Buddha's dispute with Mara over Buddha's right to sit there: here the subject of self-esteem is mentioned explicitly. Second, it is psychologically feasible that Buddha's exceedingly humble stance—in his extreme rejection of luxury and pride—is actually a compensation for an equally virulent, but more unconscious tendency to the opposite. As we have seen in the preceding chapter, the more extreme the conscious attitude is in one direction, the more extreme the opposite attitude reigns in the unconscious. Third, exposing oneself to the forces of nature and managing to withstand various natural catastrophes which then arise can easily lead anyone to feel special and even superior. The initial choice of such self-exposure is daring the forces of nature: one exposes oneself and dares God and nature to take up the challenge. Fourth, if the result of the solitary experience is any proof, Buddha's solitary experience results in his becoming a

Figure 6. "The Faust Motif," detail of "The Temptations of St. Anthony," Hieronymus Bosch (1460-1516). Lisbon: Museu Nacional de Art Antiga.

religious figure of major import. Fifth, Buddha's choice of solitude, his withdrawal from society, was a conscious choice, a search for something beyond, something more elevated, more worthy than the normal world of social intercourse. All of this seems to confirm the hypothesis that temptations of grandiosity are an inherent part of the search for solitude, also as it is exemplified by Buddha's story.

But let us go on to look at Saint Anthony, whose name has become synonymous with temptation. Here it was not Mara, but the Christian Devil who visited the future saint in his retreat in the desert. What supposedly happened then has fascinated generations of artists since, the most famous being Mathias Grünewald, Albrecht Dürer, Martin Schongauer, Hieronymus Bosch, Peter Breughel, David Teniers, Velasquez, Tintoretto, Tiepolo, and, among the more modern, James Ensor, Odilon Redon, Max Beckmann, Max Ernst, and Salvador Dali. All of the works reflect the mysteriousness of the Saint's experience. The interpretation of Bosch's painting, for example, has baffled art historians to this day: there is a long list of works devoted to trying to decipher its meaning.[6] The multitude of bizarre symbols definitely gives one the impression of torment, but apart from the fact that the torment involves women and food, it is difficult to grasp just what the deeper meaning of his vision is: what exactly was Bosch trying to say about this temptation? Gustave Flaubert, who saw Bosch's work during his visit to Lisbon in 1845, was so enthralled by it that he sat down to write a piece which he called *La tentation de Saint Antoine* that he ended up working on for over twenty years.[7] Flaubert's interpretation seems to have been quite clear: the holy man of ancient Egypt was tempted by his own pride.

---

6. There are a great many books available about Hieronymus Bosch: A. Busch, *An Annotated Bibliography* (Boston: Hall, 1983); James Snyder: *Bosch in Perspective* (Englewood Cliffs, NJ: Prentice Hall, 1973); James Snyder: *Hieronymus Bosch* (New York: Excalibur, 1977); Dirk Bax, *Hieronymus Bosch* (Rotterdam, 1979); Jacques Chailley, *Jérôme Bosch et ses symboles; essal de décryptage* (Brussels: Palais des Académies, 1976); C. A. Wertheim Aymès, *Die Bildersprache des Hieronymus Bosch* (Den Hag, 1961), to name just a few.
7. Gustave Flaubert, *La Tentation de Saint Antoine*, translated by Kitty Mrosovsky as *The Temptation of St. Anthony* (London & New York: Viking/Penguin, 1983).

Flaubert portrays the hermit plagued with nocturnal visions; his guide through this adventurous night is Hilarion, a former student. Actually, Hilarion is the devil in disguise. The first thing he does is to reproach Saint Anthony, who at this point is only the humble ascetic man Anthony, with the sin of pride. The truth of this reproach becomes a shocking revelation for Anthony. At the close of his night full of visionary dreams, the self-appointed hermit is made to witness the generation of life. And he yearns to be one with the universe. We recognize here the *participation mystique* which we found in Hansel and Gretel. The symbiotic wishes for melting with the entire universe are related to the secret fantasies of his own superiority. As a witness to the generation of life on earth, Anthony is put into a position similar to that of God. Like Buddha, Anthony chose an extremely humble and solitary position. He was definitely yearning for elevation, for a transcendent experience, for something beyond the commonplace, mundane life of the world. But what lay behind this wish? May it not have been, as Flaubert, too, suggests, a yearning for a superior position, for a feeling of power, even for infinite renown in sainthood?

Whether it was, in fact, the temptation of pride, of gluttony, or sexuality, the fact remains that Saint Anthony became a renowned healer in his day. He actually has two faces which are clearly represented through his divergent pictorial representations: the one is of Anthony, the hermit, who retreated into the desert and was tempted by the devil. The other is the face of the healer who performed miracles on those who appealed to him. Significant, too, is the fact that Anthony was held in veneration as the patron of knighthood, alongside his position as patron of the poor, the sick, of domestic animals, pigs, pigherders, butchers, and brush makers. Seen as a model of knighthood, Anthony had many chapels, altars, castles and vicarages constructed in his honor.[8] An order of knights, called the Holy Order of Anthony, was even founded in 1382 by Albert von Bayern. Anthony is the prototype of the lone hero such as we know it today, be it in Raymond Chandler's detec-

8. Wolfgang Braunfels, ed., *Lexikon der christlichen Ikonographie* (Basel, Vienna, Freiburg: Herder, 1974), Vol. V.

tive hero Phillip Marlowe, or in Superman. All real heroes are basically alone.

Jesus' forty nights in the desert bear obvious similarities both to Saint Anthony's and to Buddha's retreats. He, too, led an ascetic life during this time. He fasted. He, too, was tempted by the Devil. Were the fantasies which tempted him also fantasies of his own grandiosity? Believing himself to be the son of God, he refused to make bread out of stone, to throw himself down from the pinnacle of the temple. He also refused the kingdoms which the Devil offered him. But Matthew and Luke both tell of Jesus' fame as a miracle worker from this time onward. Was this fame an ulterior motive in his solitary retreat? Clearly apparent here again, as in the preceding examples, is the search for transcendence. But perhaps Jesus also secretly harbored the wish to become the head of a new religious group and, therefore, also wished that his excellence, his incomparability be recognized by the people of his time and of the future. This would mean that the kingdoms the Devil offered him were nothing in comparison to those which he hoped to attain if he withstood the devil's temptations and continued pursuing his solitary path. He could then become the lonely hero god and this is actually what happened: abandoned by all, believed in by few, he ultimately won over masses of followers maybe just because he continued to refuse the earthly kingdoms offered him. This may sound blasphemous for many readers, but as Jesus' solitary retreat does in fact follow a tradition we have come to recognize as paradigmatic, it may nevertheless be the case.

The similarities we find in these religious myths, legends, or tales reveal some of the component elements of the temptations involved in the search for solitude. In all we see:

1. A retreat into a solitary and uncivilized place;
2. The refusal of material sustenance in the form of food and drink;
3. The refusal of spiritual sustenance in the form of human company;
4. Exposure to the forces of nature which are unleashed upon the protagonist;

5. The appearance of a figure of temptation who
6. challenges the person, especially in his sense of self-esteem,
7. and/or offers him riches;
8. The solitary acetic arises from his retreat to become an eminent religious leader, often also a healer or a miracle worker.

What does all of this mean in psychological terms? We must first consider the question in the light of the real, material conditions of these early times, when it was rare and even physically dangerous to live outside the bounds of the society. The retreat of these ascetics is not from one society to another, foreign society; it is to a place where people do not congregate—a place of wilderness, of wildness, far from civilization. These are places in which the echo of merely human voices is not to be heard. And, as we all know, far from others, in private, very private places (like, for example, in front of the bathroom mirror, when we are absolutely alone) secret fantasies can also flourish. These solitary religious figures do not need real food to replenish the body, perhaps because they feed on fantasies, on their own rich fantasies about their future fame. Another aspect connected to the fasting is the fact that, in extreme cases, it evokes trance-like states. And so, the person who thus refuses normal sustenance can very well feel set apart from the normal world and from normal people: he or she is different and somehow superior. Not needing to rely on food, one can feel quite affirmed in one's self-reliance. Grandiose fantasies of their own specialness, independence, strength are here, too, obviously one aspect of the solitary religious leader's withdrawal from the world. Parenthetically, I must mention in this context the phenomenon of fasting as it is practiced today in people with *anorexia nervosa*. This psychological illness in which normal food is refused is always accompanied by a retreat from the surrounding world (often an emotional withdrawal) and a striving for superiority—most often also in achievement.

Retreat to a solitary place was uncommon for people of the day and age of these leaders and points to the special position of he who dares to do so. Exposure to the forces of nature is, on the one hand, a realistic aspect of such a withdrawal: in the wilderness of nature there is no shelter from exposure. One hardly realizes this in the temperate climes of Europe; however, the more extreme climates in which the religious leaders we have been speaking of lived meant that going, even for a relatively short time, without shelter was something dangerous and, therefore, daring. It was like a challenge to nature, and, thus, in some way to God. On an inner psychic level, the retreat means stepping into uninhabited regions, into the unknown in which there is no protection from the wilderness. But what is the wilderness? It must be that which is beyond the bounds of society, that which has no place in society. In this specific context we can take it to mean fantasies of grandeur. We know that most cultures disdained and even punished severely a lack of modesty. The ancient Greeks spoke of *hubris,* the early Christian church of *vanitas.*

But in the history of these religious leaders, the tempter—be it the devil or Mara—is inevitably vanquished. That which he offers is in fact a temptation: it could lure the man to give up his quest for greater things, but, in fact, the wish for transcendence, for going beyond and above the normal condition of mankind is stronger and ultimately wins. What the tempter offers is not good enough, not as good as what the solitary figure foresees as his lot if he manages to withstand the temptation. Both Buddha and Jesus were offered many worlds; they refused, perhaps because they were convinced that their goals were superior: they were to become founders of immensely important religious movements if they withstood these lowly temptations. Their stories can be understood in the following way: tempted by their own fantasies of grandeur (which arise when solitude helps them to delve into unexplored regions of the psyche) they ultimately refuse to identify with them. The fantasies are a temptation against which they fight successfully. Thus, the fantasies are ultimately fulfilled.

For our purposes the repetition in all of these stories of certain motifs is of vital interest. Whether we look at these legends of divine figures or at shamanism, witchcraft, or even early medicine, we find the same basic motifs repeated again and again. The importance of solitude in the special fate of all of these special people is striking. Healers, those who bring help to the people through their connection to other spheres of existence, are generally those who:

1. Are outsiders, or at least live for a certain time outside the bounds of society;
2. Have some special relationship to other spheres of
   existence (transcendence);
3. Are, therefore, considered to be endowed with
   special healing powers.

In their solitary retreats, these people are different from the group;
they live in quite other conditions and enjoy a privileged position in
relation to the divinities. Shamans, for example, live outside the village. They are often very eccentric people. Their initiation rites also
have to do with seclusion from society. Witches, rejected by society
and often living outside the physical boundaries of the village, are
also different from the other, normal women. They were accused of
having a special relationship with the devil: that was what was
thought to make them capable of "bewitching." It's more likely
that, if these women had any special powers, it had more to do with
their knowledge of nature. Early medicine was practiced in India by
outcasts or by Jews: touching the body of another, especially a sick
or a dead person, was taboo. Anyone who did so was not fit for
normal human intercourse. Such people were banned from normal
society, but also consulted in times of ill health. Judaism reversed
these values, saying that those who care for the dead are especially
honorable people. But this in no way contradicts what we have
been saying. These people are honorable because they take upon
themselves the task of caring for that which is tabooed. It is a good
deed, a "mitzvah," for example, to wash the dead, and it is accordingly honored—both in this world and in the next.

The special connection of shamans, witches, and doctors to
nature was an essential aspect of their healing powers. And the fact
that they lived in a more exposed position, or in closer connection
to nature is an important part of the connection. Buddha, Jesus,
and St. Anthony were all able to withstand the forces of nature;
shamans, witches, and doctors made use of the forces of nature in
herbs and potions in order to heal or to curse. The "medicine" of
nature was their domain: its powers were familiar to them and
could be used at their will. Such solitary healer figures were in their
element in nature: it was their element; that is, they were thought

to live in complete harmony with nature, even in a *participatio*, or symbiosis, as we would say today. The banal world of society and normal human intercourse was something rather foreign to them. This means that the transcendent spheres were closer to Jesus and the shamans, for example, as the immanence of life: a deeper and more intimate relationship with spiritual powers belongs to the healing capacities of the solitary healers. From this healer quality we arrive at the fantasies of grandeur: this time projected onto the healers by the people. Perhaps it was the rejection of these fantasies, the refusal to identify with them which actually made these men and women different from others, special and, therefore, elevated to the role of religious leaders.

Perhaps the most impressive example of this phenomenon is its romanesque opposite which Joseph Conrad so well portrays in *Heart of Darkness*. Here the obviously very intelligent and gifted Kurtz has gone off into the wilderness at the behest of his colonial employers. In the solitude and silence of this wilderness he falls prey to his own visions of grandeur: this is what was lurking there for him. As he says himself at the tragic end of his solitary quest:

> "I had immense plans [...] I was on the threshold of great things," he pleaded in a voice of longing, with a wistfulness of tone that made my blood run cold.[9]

He becomes some kind of a magical white witch doctor, so venerated by the local natives that they become his vassals, who invoke him like a god. In the depths of the uncivilized jungle, powers of darkness are lurking—in a religious context one would just say the Devil. As the narrator of the story, Marlowe, says:

> How can you imagine what particular region of the first ages a man's untrammeled feet may take him into by the way of solitude—utter solitude without a policeman— by the way of silence—utter silence, where no warning

---

9. Joseph Conrad, *Heart of Darkness* in *The Portable Conrad*, Morton Dauwen Zabel, ed. (New York & London: Viking/Penguin, 1976), p. 585.

voice of a kind neighbor can be heard whispering of
public opinion.[10]

This is the unchallenged domain of which Cowper spoke (chapter
1, p. 37). In being "master of all one can see" lies the implicit danger of being so taken up with this unchallenged position that it goes
to one's head. As we saw in *Hansel and Gretel*, one's own unconscious fantasies can then flourish. But Kurtz is not capable of
putting his grandiose and quasi-divine self-images in their place, he
cannot shove them into the oven. Rather he lives them out in the
here and now, succumbing to them. Perhaps the religious leaders of
old, in comparison to Kurtz, were better able to use their grandiose
fantasies as white witch doctors: most became healers or wonder
workers for their grateful followers. Out of these acts of charity
grew their renown.

The search for solitude today is generally profane.
Nevertheless, the solitary fantasies, for example, of couples in love,
or of isolated artists, do reveal definite spiritual overtones. But
before going into this aspect of the search for solitude today, let us
look at the less common cases of the religiously-oriented search in
our day and age.

RELIGIOUS RETREAT TODAY

·∽·

Recent years have shown a
revival of the practice of retreat. An outgrowth of Catholic tradition, although we have seen its pre-Christian roots in the examples
of Moses and Buddha, the retreat was initiated by Garcia de
Cisneros, a Benedictine Abbot of Montserrat who lived from 1544
to 1610. It was known as *exercitia spiritualia*, a way of renewing
one's spiritual life. In a world as profane and busy as ours, there is
little time or space allowed for solitude, in the sense of time for
reflection or meditation. Similarly, there is relatively little interest in

---

10. *Heart of Darkness*, p. 560.

spiritual renewal. Nevertheless, the rebirth of the retreat seems to be pointing to a growing need among some relatively few members of the contemporary population, a need for more spirituality, or at least spiritual replenishment. Such retreats can, in fact, be valuable and nourishing. They can also, however, be used as an excuse for not confronting all of those uncomfortably real problems, especially those involving human relationships, which we are faced with in the everyday world. Spiritual retreat, as any kind of retreat, can become a socially legitimate means of avoiding conflict. As a flight into solitude, it then enables one to underline and defend one's own differentness from others: lurking in the background are fantasies of grandiosity and also deeply unconscious symbiotic desires that are often then projected onto nature. One religious form of a search for solitude is relatively popular today, although it does not primarily appear to be motivated by a search for solitude: the formation and joining of religious sects. The spiritual retreat or isolation of the group need not be physical, but often the sect and its members set themselves apart from the rest of society. On the one hand, they thus enjoy a position of separateness and, therefore, of specialness (cf., the solitary diamond). On the other hand, setting themselves apart also promotes the adhesion of the members to the group: the strong interdependence of the members who are separated off from the rest of the world makes for a symbiotic relationship in which expectations of consensus and harmony pervade. The fanaticism which often reigns has to do with the hegemony (the "Absolutheitsanspruch") of the sect and its values. This position helps the members feel superior: we can dare to be different and alone, and are, therefore, superior. The group often has the unconscious goal of bolstering, even of salvaging, the self-esteem of its members, who frequently are people with an unstable sense of identity and self-esteem. The very isolation of the group, setting itself apart from the world, prepares the ground for attaining such an elevated position. We see here to what extent such sects resemble (they even seem to be modeled on) the example of early religious leaders who set themselves off from the rest of humanity by going out into the wilderness for some time.

At the present time, the Western world is also witnessing a certain revival of Eastern religious traditions. Europeans and

Americans have recently been getting involved with Eastern meditation techniques, and often seek retreat in this context. I would like to go on here to tell the story of a man I shall call Gerry, who had practiced Zen meditation for several years before he turned to psychoanalysis. His deeper psychological motivations were, as we shall see, much in line with what I have been discussing here: the retrieval of a sense of self-worth, the search for communion with nature as a reaction to feeling unsupported and unappreciated by his milieu, and as a means of withdrawing from painful social contacts because of deep, but unconscious needs for warmth that had not been fulfilled, and that he feared could not possibly be fulfilled. Gerry's first hours with me were devoted to the praise of Zen and the criticism of analysis. He spoke of himself in the context of Zen meditation and exclusively in this context. It was as if he only existed as a practitioner of and believer in Zen meditation. Zen offered him a goal—becoming one with the universe—and a moral framework telling him how he should live and act.

Gerry clearly felt that this Eastern method of meditation had deep meaning in his life, but it was actually much more important for him than he could imagine at this point in his analysis. He felt that it calmed him and gave him worthy goals. But, Gerry was still a nervous man: he had several ticks, like swinging his foot and scratching his face as he talked. He found the Zen goal of concentrating on the here and now helpful for his professional attitude. His work as the head of a firm of commercial artists was very stressful, and he did not particularly like the work. By sitting and meditating at least two hours a day, he tried again and again to empty himself of all of the stress that built up in him in the course of a day. He also tried, in accordance with the Zen teachings, to concentrate on his work and to avoid distracting thoughts and activities. But Gerry's very unconscious motivations for the practice of Zen meditation were very revealing and had much to do with those essential points we have seen as dominant in the search for solitude: a search for absence of conflict, a search for feelings of superiority, and a search for a symbiotic relationship with Mother Nature. These sought-after qualities were meant to compensate for a less than satisfying feeling about himself, his own worth, a naive expectation of goodness in the world which was constantly disappointed, and a negative early

again to attain some sense of belonging. He also pursued his Zen ambitions for communion with the universe. He felt the contradiction, but could not consciously admit it.

Gerry's search for solitude reflects, on an individual level, those elements we have looked at earlier in religious solitary figures. His symbiotic wishes for communion with the universe and his grandiose fantasies, however, compensate for psychological needs—low self-esteem and his feeling rejected and denigrated by others. Both are symptoms of a narcissistic disturbance and point to a deep, but relatively unconscious, need for reassurance and love. As long as these needs go unrecognized and are not taken seriously, Gerry's effort to find solace—whether in Nature, in Zen meditation, or in material success—must go in vain. The process of analytical psychotherapy, especially as it brings him to reflect upon himself so he can rescue his deeper self from its isolation, may help him retrieve a sense of himself and a sense of not being alone and unappreciated. Then, perhaps, solitude can take a more human and wholesome place in his life. His Zen meditation can then, hopefully, become one relatively conscious means of dealing with lacks that he recognizes as his.

Gerry's case is definitely not exceptional. Many people seek some form of meditation or other activities with similar goals to Gerry's. They practice, for example, a sport or a hobby which requires hours of practice alone under relatively arduous conditions. They need to bolster their sense of self-esteem, to avoid conflict with others, to find communion with nature, or music, or animals. Needless to say, not all eccentric interests practiced with fervor and in solitude are necessarily used for these purposes, but many are. The essential aspect which is destructive is the unconsciousness of the goals. Once a person realizes that he or she needs this form of solitary and often egocentric activity, then the ties to it are loosened; the person becomes more flexible and ready to open up to his or her needs on a more direct, inner level. The needs have to be recognized as such in order for any maturation to be able to take place. We saw this in *Hansel and Gretel*, too. Not all forms of retreat need serve as a compensation for psychic needs that go unrecognized. But some do.

THE CULTIVATION OF SOLITUDE: AN HISTORICAL OVERVIEW

◌‍᷄

More common in our day and age is the profane search for solitude. But a look at the historical perspective on this question will show that *both* religious and profane searches for solitude have a tradition of their own. Every historical age has cultivated its own specific image of solitude. I shall be sketching out here the prototypical images and styles of solitude in the various historical epochs, going on from there to point out some factors which are typical for all. Afterward we shall be delving into the contemporary search for solitude and the psychological motives which seem to be underlying this search. Case examples from my analytical practice will help to illustrate this material.[11]

The Renaissance marks the moment when laymen first began to express an interest in solitary retreat. Petrarca completed his *De Vita Solitaria* in 1346. In it he tells why he seeks and rejoices in solitude: he loves books, denigrates the taste of the masses and wants to develop his own, individual personality. Petrarca seeks solitude in order to develop his individuality. But this does not mean that he lives like a hermit, in asceticism. He takes pleasure in being in isolated countrysides, bucolic scenes which provide the proper backdrop for his state of mind. The importance of the natural setting is a quasi-universal element in the search for solitude. But the Renaissance is typified by what we might call a humanistic search for solitude: it does not despise men and culture, although the taste of the masses is denigrated. The goal is less *away* from the others but rather *toward* oneself. The Renaissance view of solitude is in sharp contrast to that of the Middle Ages when the focus was exclusively on the religious sphere; religious people withdrew in order to seek communion with God, in order to attain to a transcendent sphere of existence. But, following the Renaissance, the

---

11. For the historical perspective here, I am greatly indebted to Renate Möhrman's book, *Der vereinsamte Mensch: Studien zum Wandel des Einsamkeitsmotivs im Roman von Raabe bis Musil* (Bonn: Bouvier, Herbert Grundmann, 1976).

tone once again becomes more religiously-oriented. People of the Baroque period sought to flee the decadence of worldliness. In solitude they punished themselves for the transgression of worldliness and prayed for forgiveness. Andreas Gryphius' sonnet "Einsamkeit," for example, places the poet in the wilderness:

> In dieser Einsamkeit der mehr denn öden Wüsten
> Gestreckt auff wildes Kraut an die bemosste See:
> Beshau' ich jenes Thal und dieser Felsen Höh'
> Auff welchem Eulen nur und stille Vogel nisten.

> *In the solitude of this more than bleak desert*
> *Spread out over wild weeds by a mossy lake*
> *I behold that valley and the heights of these rocks,*
> *The nesting place of ewes and quiet birds*

From this distanced perspective he can well see and bemoan the fate of mankind, of rich and poor, who are all subject to the sin of false pride, "vanitas":

> Hir fern von dem Pallast; weit von dem Pövels Lüsten.
> Betracht ich: wie der Mensch in Eitelkeit vergeh'

> *Here, far from the palace, far from the*
> *   lusts of the mob*
> *I contemplate how mankind wastes away in vanity*

For without the support of God, everything and everyone must necessarily stumble:

> Alles, ohne ein Geist den Gott selbst hält müss
> wanken.[12]

> *Anything without God-given spirit must falter*

---

12. Andreas Gryphius (1616-1664), "Einsamkeit" [Solitude] is included in Volker Meid, ed., *Gedichte und Interpretationen, Band I: Renaissance und Barock* (Stuttgart: Philipp Reclam jun.), p. 231. This translation is mine.

In this pessimistic and inimical view of life on earth, solitude appears as the ideal perspective from which one can view and reflect on the vanities of the world. Implicit in the hermit-like flight into solitude is obviously a certain self-aggrandizement of the solitary figure doing the observing and judging. He is far from and also above it all.

Solitude takes on quite the opposite tone during the following Rococo period. Strangely enough, this period—characterized by sensual enjoyment—also cherished solitude, but naturally saw it in quite a different way. Here people retired—not alone—but with a small, select group of friends and acquaintances to revel in the seclusion of nature. Or a couple in love retreated to a friendly and sunny scene in nature. The bucolic scenes of Antoine Watteau's paintings[13] well illustrate the atmosphere of sensual enjoyment evoked by this rather nonprivate, seemingly unsolitary seclusion in nature. Nature plays an important role as the befitting background for frolicking people who are obviously enjoying themselves and their excursion into nature. Novel here are the facts that 1) the retreat is not meant for one person alone, but rather for a small, exclusive group, and, 2) this is a sunny nature, an inviting scene, to which the people withdraw, not one leading to feelings of transcendence or melancholy, communion with greater spheres of meaning, or empathic moments of fusion. Nature has become the goal of an excursion into another enjoyable realm, perhaps in the way we regard vacations or a walk in the country on a Sunday afternoon. And so, the Rococo period would be the historical model for what people most commonly today associate with seclusion in nature.

The Enlightenment is marked by two distinct tendencies, the one religious, the other profane. During this period the Pietists retired to live in brotherhoods, secluded communities where they sought a solitary life in which they tried to cultivate a spiritual communion with God. The profane form of retreat into solitude was, as in the preceding period, a relative solitude, this time for brief periods and as a replenishment from the strains of life in society.

---

13. For example, his "Gallant Recreation" includes five or six couples courting, singing, and dancing, in a group, but also alone.

This is the way J. G. Zimmermann spoke of solitude in his important treaty *Ueber die Einsamkeit* (1785).[14] Perhaps this is the period which bears the most similarities with ours: we, too, tend to seek periods of respite from the strains of social contact in brief excursions into the solitude of nature. One impressive and loquacious example of a solitary retreat from society in this period is that of Jean-Jacques Rousseau. We shall be looking into his story in detail in the pages to follow, for he seems to provide a model for many of what I like to call the "wounded retreats" of today. Rousseau retreated from society into the solitude of the rural countryside in order to reflect on himself and his life. He spent his time here studying nature and searching his soul, trying to understand himself and what he had experienced in society. His deeper, less conscious motives were definitely the search for consolation of a wounded soul who felt hurt, offended, denigrated by his contemporaries. He longed to be understood, respected, and admired; instead he felt despised and rejected. This led him straight into the arms of Mother Nature. Rousseau's prolonged and repeated flights from the evils of the city of Paris and its society (for example, for L'Ermitage, then for the castle of Montmorency, later for Montlouis, and then for small Swiss villages) is not typical of his period. People of the Enlightenment were rather known to indulge in brief sorties into the solitude of nature. The retreat was meant as a healthy, regenerating pause at the oasis of solitude for otherwise very socially-oriented people. The period also devoted its energies to the construction of just the right architecture necessary to set the mood for its retreats. Marie Antoinette, for example, had little country houses built for herself and her courtiers. They were to be the perfect backdrop for the courtiers' games of shepherd and shepherdess. Duke Karl Eugen had a palace built near Stuttgart: it was meant for his retreats and was accordingly called "Solitude." Tea pavilions, country homes for the nobility (like Madame d'Epinay's L'Ermitage, where Rousseau spent most of his time in 1756 and 1757), hunting retreats and hermitages are all typical housing built at this time

14. J. G. Zimmermann, *Ueber die Einsamkeit*, 4 vols. (Leipzig: Weidmann, 1784-1785).

Figure 7. "A Walk at Dusk," C. D. Friedrich (1774-1840). Private collection.

specifically to satisfy the period's predilection for solitude, or what they called solitude.

But the end of the century sees quite a definite change of note. For the early Romantics, solitude has a melancholy flavor. Abandoned lovers would retreat into their solitary suffering, but actually wallowed, perhaps even reveled in this mood. And couples would retreat together into the solitary beauty of nature. The backdrop in nature is complemented by an affinity for newly constructed ruins and old graveyards. The first half of the 19th century becomes addicted to "Weltschmerz": the world as such is all too prosaic, and so, elevated spirits must opt for solitude. The ideas of Schopenhauer provide the philosophical background of such views. The life goal to be attained exclusively through solitude is self-sufficiency and self-development. As the world is devoid of meaning, nothingness is preferable. Nietzsche's ideas were influential toward the middle and the end of the century. Feeling himself to be a philosopher and a hermit by instinct, he declared solitude his home, his pure and beneficial home. The painting "Isolation," by Fernand Khnopff, well illustrates the nostalgic search for solitude so well known in the symbolist period in the wake of Nietzsche.

The 19th century knows more differentiated images of solitude than any of the preceding centuries. From the sentimental tones of the beginning of the century the tendency changes to nihilistic tones. The world of normal human intercourse becomes too banal and must be rejected in favor of a solitary retreat. The person who chooses such a solution is necessarily a superior person who has nothing in common with the masses. Here again the intimate relationship between solitude and grandiose fantasies reappears. Nietzsche's superman must necessarily be a solitary figure. Even the Romantics' melancholy bitter-sweet retreat had to do with the superiority of their sensitivity: the superior sensitivity of the Romantic soul could be cultivated only in solitude, far from the masses, far from the banalities of everyday life.

Before going on to look at contemporary images of solitude, let us sum up what we have seen here and point out the common factors which reappear throughout time. One basic element common to all profane searches for solitude since the Renaissance at least, is the desire to find and assert one's individuality, the search

Figure 8. "Isolation," Fernand Khnopff (1858-1921). Munich: Bayerische Staatsgemaldesammlungen.

for more intense contact with and further development of oneself. Petrarca represents the first generation of such men. But, five hundred years later Nietzsche, too, stresses the importance of the individual's isolation for the further development of his individualism. From this point of view the world of everyday life appears inferior: other spheres of existence, other values are sought. Nature is the chosen background for all solitary existences, except perhaps for the Romantic poets who also retreated to their garrets. Asceticism is often the predilection. However, on a less ascetic and idealistic note, we have also seen the possibility of reveling in the joys of nature. Interesting is the varying proportions of solitude: generally it is one person alone who retreats into solitude, but, it can also be a couple or even a relatively small group—a country party. The retreat to a solitary stance in nature after being hurt, often in a love affair, is a theme which runs through many idealizing images of solitude. One of the earliest examples of such an experience is Petrarca. He actually speaks mostly of his lofty, individualistic goals, but the role of his unrequited love for Laura as the less conscious motivation for his solitary retreat is probably just as important.

THE CHOICE OF SOLITUDE TODAY

∾·

The 20th century, and especially the last twenty-five years of this century, knows a highly refined culture of solitude. We have the Singles' Society, the newer yet "being together but living apart" form of society; people are doing *exercitiae* (religious retreats) or going off for meditative retreats with less religious overtones. There is the not yet old tradition of the Lilly tank, the coffin-like tank filled with the warm saline solution which people paid to lie down in and really "get into" the experience of solitude. Maybe even Bungee jumping can be seen in this light—the individual alone, jumping off into the deeps, confronting the solitary fears for his or her life. And no self-respecting individual today admits without blushing that he or she has never lived alone, that they cannot and really do not like the idea, or even the fantasy, of living alone. The capacity to be an independent person and to live alone, depending on no one and no thing is the exclusive ideal of our times. And, in fact, more people actually do live alone than ever before in history. (The first chapter delves more into the gradual relinquishment of social bonding in our world.) A similar type of independence is evident in the extraordinary skepticism with which people approach medication: feeling dependent on medication is anathema for many people today. The prevalence of a culture of solitude is the flip side of the suffering from solitude that is so widespread today, too.

We definitely live in a period in which individualism is a highly prized ideal. Yet, there are many contradictions to this ideal: a great deal of uniformity and conformism marks our times. Nevertheless, individualism remains an ideal to be striven for. But, whenever a value is highly prized by society this reflects the other, less conscious side; it tells us something about the unconscious factors underlying and determining the situation. What could this striving for autonomy that we consciously regard so highly really be about? I believe that we are actually trying to avoid deep-seated fears of dependency, that we are trying to avoid things that we fear can happen to us if we are too dependent. We can be rejected and feel hurt; we can be disappointed in the other person's lack of commitment; we can feel hindered in our development because complying to the other's wishes in order to be accepted and loved feels more important than being ourselves. Negative fantasies about dependency obviously stem from disappointments in real life dependency relationships. A sadness which has not really been lived out or expressed about not having been able to depend on important relationships leads to an understandable wariness of dependency; and yet, we must not forget all the while that it is dependency which created societies. It is quite understandable that children from broken homes are skeptical about strength and dependability—the reliability—of relationships. Also, children who have lost a parent early in life can react in a similar fashion. Even when parents stay together a child can experience unreliable parenting: whether there be too much conflict between the parents or whether one or both parents is him/herself unreliable. As a result, the future adult will have had a negative image of what dependency in relationships is all about. This person will grow up to be skeptical about, perhaps even totally reject, such relationships. But this also means rejecting relationships per se, for all relationships comprise an element of dependency. Even if I choose to "be together but live apart " (a new form of relationship often cultivated in very modern societies), I depend on the reliability of my partner, for example, to be on time, to meet me at the appointed place, to comply with what we have arranged.

As I have already mentioned, today more than ever, it is feasible, from a material point of view, at least, to live independently: most women do not need men to support them. Smaller family units are feasible; one can even choose to live alone, as many "singles" do today. Few of us really "need" a partner to survive economically. Nevertheless, dependency relationships are important building blocks of society because they have to do with our need to need people. As the folk songs of old and the popular songs of today still state, everybody needs to need or to love someone. But it is exactly this needing and not needing, wanting to rely and being afraid of relying, that is a basic and unresolvable existential contradiction for contemporary men and women.

The case of Mary Ann, as I shall call her, is significant in this context. An independent woman who knows what she wants: this is the impression Mary Ann makes. Dressed with taste and originality, she enters my office and proceeds to describe her self-sufficient life style. She is doing a demanding job at the head of an important international company. And then she pauses to say, "But wait till you hear this! All of this is endangered because I have fallen in love." The new relationship is "terribly satisfying," but also "terribly frightening." Mary Ann thought that it would actually be easier for her to give up the relationship than to integrate this man into her life.

Actually, after several sessions it became clear to her that she was worried that if she really did let this man enter her life and make a difference in it, then she had to reckon with the possibility that he could abandon her; and that would cause her too much suffering. They might have a fight about something and if she stood up for herself, he would leave her. Mary Ann could not imagine a partner being loving and stable, allowing her to think differently and stay with her nevertheless. Her fantasies about a dependent love relationship stemmed from her family life. In her memory her parents never fought, but her older brother (only two years older) did remember family quarrels. She had been very attached to her father who died when she was 12. As she said, for her "the world fell apart then." Mary Ann's fear of abandonment was born when her father died; at this time her wishes for a loving relationship went underground. She became very independent and this had always been her conscious goal: to become a woman who needed no one, never to marry, to be strong and efficient, self-sufficient and satisfied with her life, her work, and herself. Beneath all of this insistence upon autonomy, however, lay a much less conscious fantasy image of an ever-loving, ever-empathic lover. Convinced that such a man could never exist, but still secretly hoping to find him, Mary Ann swore off men and relationships. She consequently quickly became dissatisfied with any and all men she met. Thus, no friendship with a man ever lasted very long. Mary Ann also had to leave her partners before they left her. She explained this to herself as having to stand up for her own needs and wishes. When any conflict on this subject arose, she felt obliged to assert her autonomy: there was no question, she "just had to" leave. But when Mary Ann met "Gregory" things changed. Here was a man who allowed her to be and did not even protest too loudly when she stated her needs for autonomy. She seemed to have found the ideal partner: of course, it was questionable for her if he could keep up this track record. Maybe it was better to give him up rather than end up being disappointed by him, as was inevitable. He could not possibly remain the ever-loving prince she needed him to be.

SOLITUDE IN A SCHIZOID WORLD
⌖

Mary Ann's story well illustrates a problem typical of our times: an almost fanatical desire for self-sufficiency is combined with and compensates for a very unconscious wish for a symbiotic relationship. On the practical level this means that a need for devoting oneself to another combines with a terrible dread of the self-same situation. In psychological terms, we speak of a *schizoid personality*, a person who is split between his or her ambivalent needs for distance and for proximity to other people.

Fritz Riemann said that our world is schizoidizing[15]: it is marked by schizoid traits and tends to make people schizoid. Riemann observed a trend in the early 1970s that has continued and even become more severe: a world in which social relations are disintegrating, in which social structures are crumbling. Tribal structures gave way to villages, villages to extended families, extended families to nuclear families. Now even the nuclear families are shaken. And massive national structures are falling apart—for example, the Communist Block, the Soviet Union, Eastern Europe. But, the basic problem is an inner one: a schizoid person is split in the sense of being cut off from from his or her own emotional life. He or she does not feel emotional reactions to people or to things, but rather observes facts. In this way any true contact with the inner world is avoided. This avoidance necessarily extends to the outer world, to the world of relationships with people especially. Necessarily, feelings of loneliness arise.

On the level of the individual, this schizoid type of reaction is a direct result of disappointment in relationships. The person withdraws from the source of the wounding, as well as from the poten-

---

15. Fritz Riemann, *Die schizoide Gesellschaft* (Munich: Christian Kaiser, 1975). He was a German analyst (1902-1979) interested in Jungian theory and astrology, best known for his book, *Grundformen der Angst* (Munich: Masselle, 1975). He also wrote *Grundformen helfender Partnerschaft* (Munich: Pfeiffer, 1974), and *Lebenshilfe Astrologie* (Munich: Pfeiffer, 1976).

Figure 9. "The Embrace," a detail from "The Kiss of the Entire World," Gustav Klimt (1862-1918). Vienna: Österreichische Galerie.

tial source of the wounding. But, being human, a need for relationship pervades. It cannot, however, be fulfilled in a satisfying manner, for the needs are correspondingly extreme. It is actually less a need for a mature and satisfying relationship with another mature person, but rather a deeply unconscious longing for a state of melting, oneness, fusion, for feeling understood without words. We saw these needs in *Hansel and Gretel*.

Klimt's painting on page 103 shows the kind of proximity longed for by such a personality. "The Kiss of the Entire World" dates from 1891, the symbolist period, and well expresses the image of the words of the French symbolist poet, Arthur Rimbaud, in his poem, "Une Saison en Enfer" in *Délires II*. Fusion in joy is "la mer allée avec le soleil" (the ocean melting into the sun), and it is exactly this image which is painted behind the heads of the embracing lovers; they bathe in the same waters (the water laps around their feet); their heads are melting together. The sun and the moon are behind their heads and are as if flowing together in some undifferentiated waters. This is a situation of oneness, of lack of differentiation, of the uroboros (the snake biting its own tail) and the vegetative life processes. In the background an egg is being fertilized by sperm and the sperm seem to be flowing down, like rain, over the heads of the lovers. In contrast, Fernand Khnopff's woman is alone, above her head a bust of the goddess Athena, the goddess of wisdom and, therefore, of differentiation (page 97). Three separate and rather dried out tiger lilies form the foreground. This is an image of autumn, of a melancholic but in no way unpleasant solitude.

THE BACK TO NATURE TREND

∽

The 20th century knows all of these images of solitude and more. One major current which is very widespread today dates back to Jean-Jacques Rousseau, perhaps even, ultimately, to Petrarca. Both poets withdrew from society, seeking to discover and cultivate their individualism in retreat. As I have mentioned earlier, Petrarca's rejection by Laura seems to have been a major determining factor in his retreat. The poet first saw and fell in love with Laura on April 6, 1327, in the church of St. Clare in Avignon; his pure and unrequited love for this married woman became a main theme in his life. Laura died of the plague in 1348 while Petrarca was in Northern Italy. In his *Brief an die Nachwelt* [*Letter to Posterity*], he describes this love himself:

> In my youth I suffered from a burning love, a simple and honorable love. And I would have suffered longer still had not a bitter, but beneficial death put out the fire that was already dying down.

At this point in his life, as his German editor says:

> [F]earful and bitter, he gave himself over to an ill-humored weariness of life and let the middle years of life express his melancholy. For many years he continued to torture himself thus, and vainly sought relief: even in the jubilee year 1350 when he made a pilgrimage to Rome, and then in his customary solitude in Vaucluse.[16]

Vaucluse is significant in Petrarca's life as the place to which he retired (1337) in an effort to put a certain distance between himself and Laura (who lived in Avignon) and, thus, to find some peace of mind. It was here that he first took up the solitary style of life which led him to write, in the early spring of 1346, his now famous treatise *De Vita Solitaria*.[17] Here the poet praises books in his efforts to find a sense of himself, to distinguish himself from the masses. It is definitely in view of his own search for developing his own individualism—and not in search for a transcendent experience with God—that Petrarca sought solitude. The other aspect of his search was a less conscious one, the search for consolation from his unrequited love for Laura, for his pain.

---

16. These two quotes are from Hans W. Eppelsheimer, ed. *Petrarca, Dichtungen, Briefe und Schriften* (Frankfurt: Insel Verlag, 1980), pp. 28, 15.
17. Francesco Petrarca, *The Life of Solitude*, translated by Jacob Zertlin (Westport, CT: Hyperion Conn., 1985, reprint of 1924 edition).

In one of his *epistolae metricae*, addressed to Giacomo Colonna, we learn of the life the poet led here in Vaucluse and of the importance of Laura, of her absence, in his inner life. Petrarca obviously sought comfort, on the one hand, in nature and, on the other, in books. But a less conscious aspect of his retreat was definitely largely determined by the fact that his love for Laura found no satisfaction in reality.

This very early example of retreat into solitude is exemplary: it is the first documented search for solitude for other purposes than religious. Its conscious motivation is a superior image of oneself and its less conscious motivation is an escape from hurt feelings: it is meant to calm the pain caused by rejection. The combination with a higher ideal—that of finding one's own individualism—is quite typical even for such retreats today. One could argue that Petrarca's retreat to Vaucluse was not really solitary, for he did see friends and did not live in complete seclusion from society. He actually lived in the middle of a city. But, from his point of view, he was living in solitude. And, in fact, it was a relative solitude, for his life both before and after his seclusion in Vaucluse was marked by extreme involvement in social contacts and obligations.

In a similar but more definitely pathological vein, we find—five hundred years later—the very influential example of Jean-Jacques Rousseau. This French poet, of the time of the Enlightenment, who is a very early precursor of the Romantic era, retreated to solitude in nature. His motivation was quite clearly his suffering from rejection: Rousseau felt hurt, unjustly criticized and rejected by his contemporaries. Critics today speak of delusions of persecution. He speaks of this experience in detail in his works, for example in his *Les Confessions de Jean-Jacques Rousseau*. As the editors of this work remark in their first footnote to this lengthy volume, "When he wrote these lines, between 1766 and 1770, Rousseau believed he was the victim of a conspiracy directed against him."[18] In 1756, Rousseau sought out a natural retreat in

18. My edition is Jean-Jacques Rousseau, *Die Bekenntnisse, Les Confessions*, in *Oevres complètes* (Paris: Editions du Seuil, 1967).

Madame d'Epinay's l'Ermitage, and from this position of solitude, which was actually life in the country, in relative seclusion, he expounded on the joys and the natural goodness of nature. He lived, together with his wife and mother-in-law, in L'Ermitage, a little country house which Madame d'Epinay lent him. Here he wrote many of his renowned works, *La Nouvelle Héloise, la Lettre à d'Alembert sur les Spectacles, le Contrat Social*,[19] in which he develops the theoretical background for his belief in the beauty and goodness of nature and the natural man, "le bon sauvage" (the good savage), and the comparative evil and degeneration of society and the life of civilization. Naturally here he finds justification for his hatred of the acts and judgments of his imagined persecutors. What Rousseau actually does is to rationalize his hurt by constructing a whole sociological and philosophical theory that serves to justify himself and his own position and to vilify his enemies. This is neither new nor surprising. What is astounding is the impact his views had on succeeding generations. Or do the representatives of the "back to nature movement" re-invent Rousseau each time anew? Is his attitude, or is what we might call "the Rousseau phenomenon" a typically human, or perhaps a typically modern, way of reacting to pain suffered in society?

In order to try to understand the deeper psychological motivations underlying Rousseau's love of solitude we must examine his early life. His mother died just after his birth; he says that he felt responsible for her death: "I was born weak and sick; I cost my mother her life, and my life was the first of my misfortunes." A very sensitive child with an excitable temperament, he says of himself, "I felt before I could think. This is the common fate of humanity. But I suffered it more than others."[20] The great passion of his life was Mrs. Warrens, a woman thirteen years older than himself, whom he called "Mama" and who called him "my little one." After some time they became lovers. Rousseau probably sought comfort from

---

19. These works are available as: *La nouvelle Héloise,* or the *New Eloise* (University Park: PA: Pennsylvania State University Press, 1987); *Du Contrat Social,* or *Social Contract,* Maurice W. Cranston, tr. (New York: Viking/Penguin, 1968).
20. *Les Confessions* in *Oevres complètes,* Preface by Jean Fabre. (Paris: Editions du Seuil, 1967), Book I, 3: p. 22. My translation.

his lack of a mother in the lap of Mother Nature and in the *ersatz* mother, Mrs. Warren. As we see from the way he reacted to the world around him, Rousseau seems to have cherished idealistic and unrealistic images of himself and of relationships He felt persecuted by the literary and philosophical circles of his day: they did not provide him with the understanding which he desperately needed from an all-accepting, maternal environment. And so, he fled into the consoling lap of Mother Nature; here he could feel, or at least unquestioningly fantasize, the symbiotic connection—the melting with the world around him, fusion with the archetypal mother. Here we have once again the world of Hansel and Gretel, but this time the evolution to realistic, mature adulthood does not take place. In fact, Rousseau gets lost permanently in the wilderness of nature, in the domain of the witch, for he does not manage to develop a sense of relatedness to the world around him. He does try very hard, searching his soul in several autobiographical pieces, a procedure decidedly meant to help him shed some light on himself. He also writes a treatise on child education, *Emile*, but, in the end, all is of no use. Instead of finding himself, he buries himself more and more in his fantasies of persecution. He does not raise his own biological children as he suggests that Emile be brought up. Instead he gives them up to an orphanage at birth! The idealistic visions which are expounded in his treatises (as *Emile*) belong to the realm of the white bird (cf. page 47 ff., chapter 1). Rousseau remains a captive of the witch.

Rousseau is a direct forerunner of every "back to nature" movement since his time. The ecological movement obviously harks back to him, for here, too, nature tends to be seen and felt as all-good and society, the world of man and civilization, as all-bad. Evil men in a civilization geared for profit destroy Mother Nature who is the all-generous provider, this is the basic premise. Such a polarization of nature and culture, of civilization and nature, whereby nature stands for good, the pure, and civilization stands for evil and the sullied is a main point in Rousseau's philosophy. The expression *le bon sauvage* ("the good savage") stems from his pen.

The 19th century American writer Henry David Thoreau stands for similar principles with regard to nature and to society.

He, too, retired to a solitary place in natural surroundings, Walden pond, not far from Boston. He, too, was a person who had difficulty getting along in society, felt slighted at a whim and retreated from the stage of his suffering to find consolation in nature, in solitude, in an unchallenged position there (as did Cowper). As the editor of *Walden* writes, "From the beginning he seems to have liked being by himself."[21] When he left Harvard in 1837, Thoreau began to look for a garret, a place to get away from the hubbub of family life. The second entry in the journal which he began after completing Harvard is thus titled "Solitude." What made Thoreau so yearn for solitude? Was it his unsociable character? He was renowned for his "forced directness." Emerson said that:

> There was somewhat military in his nature not to be subdued, always manly and able, but rarely tender, as if he did not feel himself except in opposition.[22]

And so, we have on the one hand a very individual and difficult character, uncompromising and therefore, liable to feel himself not in accord with society. We can follow the theme of rejection leading to solitude in Thoreau's relationships with women: Thoreau fell in love, it seems, twice. First of all with Ellen Sewall whom he met in 1839 and lost to his brother John. Six months after she rejected him (November 1840), he moved in with Ralph Waldo Emerson and his wife, Lydian. He fell in love with Lydian, but his love seems to have been unrequited. He finally writes:

> "And now another friendship is ended. . . . I am perfectly sad at parting from you. . . . Morning, noon, and night, I suffer a physical pain, an aching of the breast which unfits me for my tasks."[23]

---

21. Henry David Thoreau, *The Portable Thoreau,* edited, with an Introduction by Carl Bode (London: Penguin, 1947, 1977), pp. 4, 12.
22. Ralph Waldo Emerson, quoted in *The Portable Thoreau*, p. 7.
23. *The Portable Thoreau*, p. 12.

Thoreau leaves the Emerson home in 1843 to take up his abode in the solitude of nature two years later.

SOLITUDE IN THE LAP OF MOTHER NATURE TODAY

·◇·

Why do so many modern, rationally oriented people since the Enlightenment so often tend to seek the solitude of Mother Nature? Is it merely the unchallenged position they relish—Cowper's reigning over all one can see? Or is something else involved? What might the phenomenon of retreat into solitude have to do with typically human patterns of behavior, to the archetypes? We have seen again and again the temptation of grandiose fantasies accompanying solitude. Might these fantasies be necessary for people in certain states? The fact is that underlying these examples of the retreat into the solitude of nature, from Petrarca to Rousseau and Thoreau, is a withdrawal from a difficult, even a painful, rejection, be it real, potential, or fantasized. The society of others reminds one of pain and suffering. Society is also the place in which one proves oneself or not, the place where one's self-worth is confirmed or not. Fantasies of grandeur or even more modest ideal images of one's own value, cannot be upheld in the face of a rejecting or even critical society. The lack of echo in society leads one to re-examine one's own images of oneself. When society has not provided enough in the way of recognition, then the fantasy of Nature provides solace: symbolically it represents the mother. This is a fact of life and has been so for thousands of years, as Erich Neumann's impressive book, *The Great Mother*,24 so well

---

24. First published in 1953, *The Great Mother: An Analysis of the Archetype,* was translated into English by Ralph Manheim for Bollingen Series, Vol. 47 (Princeton: Princeton University Press, 1964). It provides a wealth of cultural background material showing the variations in the manifestations of the Great Mother today, and in prior ages.

shows. Its acceptance is without words. One can just feel good and accepted, without the question of value even being raised. The lap of mother nature is warm, comforting, and accepting. Fantasies of fusion with nature, of the *participation mystique,* abound here. These surroundings are far from the rejection and coldness, criticism and hurt we might have experienced in the world of human interaction. One could very well say that such a retreat is basically regressive. But we all know that regression can have an absolutely positive aspect, especially if it is a conscious movement to a source of comfort.

CINDERELLA'S RETREAT, FANTASIES, AND RETURN TO RELATIONSHIP

∽·

We shall now have a look at the fairy tale *Cinderella,* for it shows a young girl who feels abandoned by all, but who actually also fears relationships; she cultivates, instead, a special relationship to nature and secret grandiose images of herself. Here we will find a recognizable, typically human pattern of behavior in which we can recognize what the temptations of solitude can look like in real life.

Cinderella is the daughter of a wealthy man; her mother dies when she is still young. Within a year of her mother's death, her father remarries. Her stepmother brings two daughters of her own along into the new family. This initial setting is similar to *Hansel and Gretel:* Cinderella has lost her real mother and has instead a cruel stepmother. Hansel and Gretel have a cruel mother. Hansel and Gretel are abandoned emotionally and led out into the woods to die. Cinderella is abandoned emotionally, too, through her mother's dying and through her father's remarrying. She is kept physically within her own, her father's own house: but here she is treated like a servant: she has to get up early, carry in the water, make the fire, cook and wash and do all the menial chores. She is made to dress like a servant, too—in an old gray jacket and wooden

Figure 10. "Cinderella," Anonymous artist. A theater poster, Glasgow, 1880. Collection de la Bibliothèque de l'Union Centrale des Arts Décoratifs.

shoes. And when her stepsisters torture her by throwing peas and lentils into the ashes of the hearth, she has to sort them out. This is how she got her name, Cinderella, because she was always covered with cinders.

In her solitude, abandoned, with no loving relationships, without a sense of belonging to a caring community or being remembered dearly by anyone, Cinderella turns to her dead mother. She cries over her mother's grave on which she has planted a branch. This is the only thing she had asked her father to bring home for her: she makes only modest demands, although deep down inside her needs are much greater. She has shed so many tears over this branch that a tree has grown up in its place. And each time she goes to cry over the grave a little white bird appears which grants her her every wish. What does this crying over the branch and the white bird mean? We have seen the white bird in *Hansel and Gretel* where it led the children to the witch's house. Here it serves as a messenger, most likely between her and her dead mother, or at least to an intermediary figure, her fairy godmother who listens to her sorrows and makes her wishes come true. Both the witch and the fairy godmother belong to the realm of the Great Mother. They are feminine figures who have special powers with regard to life itself. Cinderella's wishes are directed to her dead mother and, therefore, to the domain of the spiritual. The contact with the earth, with physical reality, with the entire realm of mother earth is deficient. Maternal abandonment is a given in both *Hansel and Gretel* and in *Cinderella*. All three children turn to the spiritual realm for solace. All three get trapped in the realm of the Great Mother, for they do not know how to deal with the reality of life. Their expectations are too grandiose and naive: Hansel and Gretel believed that paradise on earth was possible in the witch's house: they unsuspectingly pounced upon it, only to discover too late that it was an illusion. Their trap is the belief in the promises of symbiosis.

Cinderella cultivates similarly unrealistic fantasies, but they are about her own value: she wishes explicitly not for appropriate clothing to go to the ball, but for "silver and gold." And she repeats this wish on three separate occasions. This extraordinary wish is comparable in magnitude to the extraordinarily negative images associated with her day-to-day reality. Treated as a maid, she longs to be a princess. This instability may have to do with puberty: Cinderella's father is at first the sole object of her affection. When he does not pay enough attention to her, for example, by marrying another woman, she feels lowly, demeaned, like a maid who is treated poorly. When she fantasizes about herself, it is only in the highest of terms: the soiled gray mouse is a beautiful and absolutely admirable princess in her fantasies.

Here we see a clear case of unstable self-esteem and the completely opposite fantasies which it breeds. As I have mentioned in the preceding pages, an instability of the sense of self-esteem invariably has to do with a lack of the appropriate inner structures which support and guarantee a stable identity. Self-doubt is a normal and a basically healthy phenomenon. But the extreme swings of mood, from the depths of dejection to the heights of elation, are typical of narcissistic personalities. Self-worth is *the* topic of major interest in their lives. A deep and often extremely unconscious sense of solitude is also typical. These people live distant from all, feel understood by none, and cannot establish meaningful relationships, for they have no real relationship with themselves and their own feelings. Those who feel especially alone, unloved, and abandoned, especially suffer from this type of problem. But inner solitude and withdrawal from the world with a sense of hurt pride is extreme in these cases. Recovery is difficult: it takes a long time to retrieve a relatively good feeling about oneself.

We must conclude that with such a problem of self-esteem and with such a lack of supportive inner structures, it would be difficult for Cinderella to establish meaningful relationships. We see that when she meets the prince she establishes a loose relationship, based on admiration of her physical beauty. Then she flees. She withdraws into solitude, back to her cinder maid condition three times before she dares confront reality and really encounter the prince. She cannot stay in touch long enough to establish a real relationship. From the beginning she is portrayed as a person who feels her surroundings to be inimical and isolates herself from them. This is her way of perceiving the world, perhaps because her mother has died, perhaps because she does not get the attention she wants from her father. But this is all projection. It is she who cannot empathize with herself.

Cinderella looks like a little gray mouse, but inside she is yearning desperately for a prince charming who will come along and give her a sense of self-worth, or rather confirm the sense of grandeur that she secretly cherishes. Although the fairy tale does not specify her age, we can imagine that she is in puberty. This is a stage of life in which self-doubt is especially prominant. The ugly duckling has not yet become a beautiful swan, but it senses the potential within. The father is still the major masculine figure of import and rivalry with the mother for his affection is particularly intense. Rivalry is accordingly a major theme in the fairy tale: it is directed toward the stepsisters and the stepmother. They are portrayed as being jealous of Cinderella, but this is a projection. It is more likely Cinderella, herself, who rivals with them for her father's affection. And in her pain of feeling unloved, unadmired, even rejected, she flees into fantasy and bathes in her grandiose self-images. This situation reminds me of the analysand in the preceding chapter, Jane. She, too, felt rejected in being brought up in the orphanage and, in her dejection, fantasized that she was a prophetess.

Cinderella's story is interesting because of the clarity with which it shows how fantasies of grandeur can flourish alongside—and actually be—a vivid and necessary compensation for feelings of rejection and abandonment. The hope for Cinderella lies in her age: at puberty it is common, even normal, to experience this type of conflict and insecurity in the realm of self-esteem. One's own value is not clear, for one is no longer a child and not yet an adult. It is not at all evident as yet what one can and cannot do, what one is and what one is not. A sense of identity gradually becomes stabilized through experiences in the personal (and later in the professional) world and more realistic self-appraisal becomes possible. Cinderella's story would be a lot more problematic if she were not in puberty.

The developmental aspect of the tale which is of import for us in the context of the temptation of solitude has to do with Cinderella's evolution. At the beginning she is living in an unwanted solitude. Later we see that it is she who chooses a degree of solitude, or at least a degree of separation from the prince—she chooses to withdraw again and again. She must, however, own up to her standpoint, to her being also the extraordinarily beautiful girl at the ball, in order to grow up and enter into a real relationship with the prince. Here, as in *Hansel and Gretel*, the all too narrow focus on the parental figures must be broadened in order for the girl to pursue her own developmental journey.

THE TOPOS OF THE SOLITARY HERO: TRAITS AND DEVELOPMENT

ᜑ

The grandiose visions involved in solitude are quite evident here: they are easily perceived from our perspective. However, for the person who retreats into solitude, often with a feeling of hurt, or in a desperate effort to find him- or herself, this perspective must necessarily sound quite foreign. Depressive people who feel alone and abandoned not only often isolate themselves, they also often cherish in some secret part of their being fantasies of their own grandeur and even superiority. They are too good to be appreciated by their environment; when they suffer so, and perhaps even die, then the world will realize that they were really very good, worthwhile, etc. In actual fact they often cannot just die, but they can and often do "die to the world," retreating in a huff, like Rousseau, for example, very disappointed by the fact that the world has not come to recognize their special value.

The retreat from society to a solitary position is a phenomenon that goes hand in hand with fantasies of grandeur, with fantasies of being like or being in touch with divine beings, with fantasies of being or searching to be in some way superior. The retreat into solitude is obviously a retreat from relationships. This is a basic and essential point. All hero images depict a solitary hero, one who dauntingly goes from adventure to adventure with little compunction about leaving those relationships that he—or she—has established. Even the relatively recent female hero fantasies in detective novels, such as Sara Paretsky's female detective V. I. Warshawski, has little regard for relationships, getting involved and disinvolved rather easily, going on to new and better, or just different tasks, leaving one man for another with seeming ease. More important than relationships is the call of duty, the deed to be done, the heroic action to be accomplished. It seems as though such heroic deeds can only be accomplished by a solitary hero, or in this case heroine. Solitude is a basic component of hero-ness. And, conversely, the unspoken implication of all flights into solitude is the fantasy of transcending the merely human realm: the goal is the attainment of a superior, heroic, even a divine realm of superiority. Bernardin Schellenberger[25] quotes a Zen poem in which the master warns the disciple on his journey up a river not to stop for a child crying on the bank. One cannot help others until one has come to find oneself. The disciple must go on until he has found himself. Only then can he really help the crying child. Schellenberger admits that he himself did not get as far along as he would have hoped, because he frequently stopped for the child. This revelation makes us see Pater Bernardin Schellenberger perhaps as less of a solitary hero, but more of a human, or a humane person: relationships seem to mean more to him than his own heroic goal of self-discovery. And, in fact, the retreat into solitude is often idealized when the deep, underlying motivation is an avoidance of relationships, out of fear of being hurt, misjudged, criticized, or rejected.

But the image of the hero has often also been used to describe the path of human development. Erich Neumann's book on the evolution of consciousness[26] impressively uses this topic to describe the way in which the person evolves as a center of his or her own

25. Bernardin Schellenberger's essay, "Ins Gelobte Land der Großen Einsamkeit," in *Von der Kraft der Sieben Einsamkeiten*, edited by Rudolf Walter (Basel, Vienna, Freiburg: Herder, 1984), pp. 19-32.

26. Erich Neumann, *Ursprungsgeschichte des Bewusstseins*, or *The Origins and History of Consciousness*, R. F. Hull, translator, Bollingen Series, Vol. 42 (Princeton: Princeton University Press, 1954).

Figure 11. "Puberty," Edvard Munch (1863-1944). Oslo: National Gallery.

subjectivity, goes on to fight the dragon, to capture the treasure and free the princess. His description is an imposing systematization of the history of the development of human consciousness. It is the heroic figure who goes on from one developmental step to the other. This figure stands for progress and advancement, betterment, self-betterment and betterment of the human race on the level of the individual human being. In actual fact, the advance from one stage of psychic and social development to the next is often one of a heroic achievement. Nevertheless, Neumann, himself, would certainly not have hesitated to say that the heroic figure is invariably plagued with feelings of being the anti-hero: the suffering, the fears, doubts, and insecurities that he or she feels along the path of development belong to the path and to the person. In this context we can see how well Neumann understood the perils of the individual along this path, when he said: "Every time a child leaves its position of security, it feels alone and lonely."[27]

It is actually with each step in its development, with each progressive maturation of the personality and with each new and, therefore, daring situation that a child leaves a position of security for new, virgin land. In this way solitude is an unavoidable step on the way to further development. Solitude in some form or another belongs to each new life phase. Puberty is, in this respect, a model example which is worth our while to examine here, if only for the pressing reason of our contemporary adolescents' quasi-epidemic addiction to life-endangering drug consumption.

Puberty is a major transition phase and, as such, is fraught with the insecurities of the unknown. It is also, therefore, a stage of great solitude. A painting by Edward Munch ("Puberty," on page 118) shows a young girl at this time in her life. We see here many of the elements involved in the experience which, in themselves, invariably indicate feelings of being alone and lonely. The young girl is sitting on the edge of her bed, naked and seemingly ashamed of her nakedness: she holds her arms crossed in front of her, as if she were trying to shield herself from the sight of an invis-

---

27. Erich Neumann, *The Child* (Boston: Shambhala, 1990), p. 122.

ible spectator. Her position is stiff and her eyes are wide. She is staring straight out in front of her. What this means exactly we can only surmise. Is there an element of challenge, of brazenness here? Or is she just gazing out into the world that passes before her inner eye? Whatever, we definitely sense a feeling of solitude and fear; a coldness dominates the picture. The girl is hardly sitting on the bed, just sort of perched on its edge. If we try to place ourselves in the same physical position we can, at best, get a feeling for what might be going on inside. Perhaps she is afraid to get into the bed. Or maybe she is just sitting there wondering timidly about herself and her life, the new developments (both physical and psychological), which she must be noticing in herself now. At any rate there is a feeling of insecurity in this posture. Behind her left shoulder we see a huge shadow that actually flows along the whole left side of her body, from her feet to well above her head. What is this shadow? Perhaps the whole shadowy, unknown, but vaguely felt area which lies before her. She must sense something lurking there, as yet not completely known. The shadow could have to do with her body, with her sexuality, with her future life as a woman. A look at the colors the artist has chosen give us a hint of the subject matter involved here. Some spots and strokes of red, a brownish red on her cheeks, lips, and nipples seem to allude to menstrual blood, perhaps also to the blossoming of a fresh sexuality and to a blush of shame connected with it. These are the feeling tones and the matters connected with puberty. Interestingly, the girl's bed is also reddish brown, almost the same tone as the colors used on her body. This is the background color of the bed on which the girl usually lies: this means, this is the basic tone of her experience. The brown at her feet is like a carpet: this is the color of her standpoint, that is, the whole domain of mother earth, the chthonic aspect of the feminine is her position at the present time. The coloring of the painting, as well as the girl's nakedness and her position, all tell us that the girl is involved with the theme of femininity now. But she is pale as yet: her bed is yet a pristine white with tones of green, indicating something new and fresh, as yet unsoiled, perhaps like a lily. As lily white is a color often associated with virginity, I imagine that this is the precarious position on which the girl is poised. She is sitting poised on the threshold to womanhood, not yet there, but no longer a little girl. The ochre red of her face and of the background, in their earthy coloring, can indicate that these are the things lurking in her mind. But there is still a lot of fear and hesitation (the shadow on her left—unconscious—side).

All of this—the fears and the fantasies, the inklings and the observations—all of this means insecurity and reveals the extent to which this phase of life is one marked by solitude. An area of new ground, tinged with uncertainties and, hence, with solitude. A time in which one goes through enormous mental and physical metamorphoses, one is alone and isolated with the newness of one's own personal passage. However exciting or forbidden it may be to discuss the new topic of sexuality and maturity with peers, parents, or at school, one is ultimately alone in going through the experience.

Winnicott speaks of the importance of solitude at this time (as well as earlier in life). Adolescents, he says, put up defenses against being "found." This is important, for what is personal and feels real must be defended at all costs. It is precisely the development of such a capacity for isolating oneself from the environment which helps adolescents begin to become individual people in a more clear and evident way than ever before in their development. Children who do not go through such a phase of isolating themselves are too afraid to do so; they sense too much danger in such a separation. They thus tend to be and remain overadapted. But at some point in their development they must come to find the strength to retreat in order to find themselves. The danger of losing the love and admiration of their milieu, the security of their life situation becomes a definite impediment to development. The longer such a clinging to infantile values and relationships remains, the less a person dares to become him- or herself and to be, speak, dress and act differently from what they fantasize is expected of them.

This developmental problem calls to mind the story of a man I shall call Mickey, a middle-aged man who came to see me because he was suffering from depression. When Mickey was in puberty he sought solitude: he would go upstairs to the attic, put a mattress on the floor and read. He would refuse to go down to be with the family: but mealtime was a must he felt he could not refuse, so downstairs he would go; he would sit at the table with the rest of the family and either refuse to eat, or would eat infinitesimal quantities. He needed to refuse the food his mother offered him, the maternal nourishment, he needed to reject the nest warmth, the comfort of his mother's presence and care. And, at the same time, he needed to find a long neglected, thus far quite ambivalent connection with his father: he needed to find a role model for what it meant to be a man. At this time Mickey's father was on a strict diet; and Mickey's fasting was a way to be close to his father, to be like him, to identify with him. And he needed to withdraw or find his inner distance from the world of the mother. This actually was important in order for him to grow up. We can think back to Hansel and Gretel here, who needed to be abandoned in the woods in order to grow up. And so, when we think of Mickey up in his attic, refusing to partake in family life, fasting and following the white bird (in reading up in his attic) we realize that he was in a kind of incubation phase. He actually also slept a lot alone up there in his attic. Although our modern world hardly knows the custom of incubation as it is practiced by "primitive peoples" in many parts of the world, we see here that this is what Mickey was unconsciously practicing. This is a meaningful ritual for adolescents (as well as for people in other difficult life phases). As everyone knows, incubation means sitting on eggs in order to hatch them through the warmth of the body. The image is used in order to speak of the kind of withdrawal needed for concentrating one's energies on an important development to be achieved.

Many are the tribal rites for puberty in so-called primitive cultures. They all involve some kind of seclusion. Young boys are subjected to intense experiences, first being taken out of the family, away from their mothers to go through masculinity rites with a new social group—their masculine peers. They emerge as adult members of the social community, but only after having gone through a trial of sorts in which a ritual death or dismemberment has been acted out. They must die in their old roles in order to emerge prepared for their new roles. Girls' puberty rites offer even more impressive images of seclusion, for the girls are often placed alone in huts where their feet are not even allowed to touch the ground. These rites institutionalize the need to be alone which Winnicott spoke of as being all important in puberty.

The myth of Danaë, the mother of Perseus, is also a story of seclusion; it helps us understand further dimensions involved in this type of ritual. Danaë is put away, probably at puberty, because her father is afraid that the gods' prediction will be fulfilled: she is to bear a son who will kill him. Symbolically this means that Danaë is put into solitary confinement in order to protect the powers which reign from being dethroned by the powers developing within her. The role of each new generation is renewal: it must fight and defeat the old powers. On a psychological level, the myth is telling us that new tendencies are threatening to the old, and that the old try to repress the new in order to retain their power. This is a classical theme repeated again and again in the myths of many peoples, from Babylonian mythology's battle of Marduk against Apsu, to Greek mythology's battles of Zeus against his father, Cronus. It can even be seen in Christianity's repeated battles against Judaism. We can imagine that the seclusion of adolescents at puberty may have arisen as a means by which the respective society tried to protect itself against the powers brewing in the new generation. In the self-same context, the fear of menstrual blood is also a reason for not allowing the girls' feet to touch the ground: blood is especially powerful (it is actually equivalent to the power of life, itself, and, therefore, is as powerful as the gods themselves); the girls themselves, therefore, represent a danger for the prevailing powers. And, in fact, tremendous energy and vitality are unfolding in the child who is on the point of becoming an adult. So, the seclusion enforced on adolescents has a two-fold or a double-edged meaning: on the one hand, it refers to the importance of concentrating life energies on development: the energy is to be focused inside, in order to facilitate the unfolding of inner processes. On the other hand, and directly related, is the society's fear of what the adolescent's energy might lead to if left unchannelled. The results could be dangerous for society. Both interpretations can be correct, for both recognize and stress the especially potent powers slumbering in the adolescent.

The adolescent faced with all the turmoil of these years is, however, in a precarious position. The combination of tremendous energy with the sense of insecurity naturally also belonging to this stage can lead the child to turn to extreme solutions: drug and alcohol consumption, delinquency, and even suicide belong to the picture at this time in life. All seem to offer solutions, the promise of escaping an all too threatening sense of solitude, facing the confusion of this time alone. These solutions are most frequently a way of conforming to peer group pressures, and, therefore, grant a sense of belonging, of not being different and isolated from the all-important group. The adolescent can be influenced by the peer group to steal, to commit acts of vandalism, to indulge in alcohol or drug consumption. Whatever the addiction of the times, it becomes the trap of the destabilized or not yet stabilized adolescent: whether it be driving fast cars, like in the 1950s, drinking beer in the 60s, or taking drugs in the 70s. Everyone is doing it, and, in order to feel part of the group, to feel accepted and not to feel like an outsider, isolated, alone and abandoned, the adolescent conforms: he or she finds him- or herself in a community of spirits, belonging to a group and not ridiculed or rejected by the others.

Such conformity to peer groups begins early and is definitely important: the group determines which pop star is to be venerated, which brand of jeans to wear, which expressions are to be used among the members of the "in group." Paradoxically, the search for being separate and unique—the steps involved in becoming a unique individual—evolves out of a tendency to conform to new groups, outside of the family. This is a dangerous balancing act, for the more the child needs to feel accepted by the peer group (in order to attain a sense of self-esteem), the more endangered it is. When self-esteem and security have not been previously well-anchored in early experiences, then the group becomes of supreme importance: a symbiosis with the group—in place of a symbiosis with the family or the mother—is sought. Any differentiation from the group and its ideals, its standards, its specific morals (or lack of them) is threatening. The child becomes a follower, doing everything it can to retain this all-important source of satisfaction and belonging; trying to avoid with all its might any inkling of feeling so lonely and worthless. The need for peer approval is so great as to make the assertion of any individuality—now or often later—dangerous and not desirable. One very tragic aspect of this phenomenon was prevalent in various earlier epochs—suicide: Gide's young boys in *The Counterfeiters* portrays the multiple suicides of adolescents conforming to peer pressure. In our day and age the disastrous proportions of drug addiction are the result of this phenomenon.

In youth and young adulthood the effects of early solitude reveal themselves in serious problems in dealing with the Scylla and Charybdis of individualism and adaptation. During these years, which are generally ones of extroversion, of adaptation to the demands of life in the world and external reality, the tendency to introversion is naturally minimal. However, if the capacity for being alone is lacking, then the flight from solitude is accompanied by an overadaptation to the outer world.

Young adulthood is a time of unavoidable separations and experiences of solitude which can be extremely painful. Leaving home and homesickness is one side of the problem. The other is separations from friends and romantic partners. Hansel and Gretel's story offers a positive example of a developmental process leading from leaving home and solitude into a capacity for relating in the world. In recent years, we have been witnessing among young adults an incapacity for experiencing solitude that leads to a perseverance in the family situation and a persistence in this first loving relationship. Here is the witch who cannot let the children go. Solitude can be so feared that it is avoided for as long as possible. The family must persist in its security-granting role, because the person concerned is so much in need of this original source of security. Either it has not been well enough internalized or it was an unsatisfactory source of security in the first place. The basic feelings of identity, self-esteem, and, hence, security have not been well enough established; the person does not have the appropriately strong inner images that enable him or her to go on into the solitude that necessarily belongs to leaving home.

C. G. Jung is especially known as the psychoanalyst who appreciated the importance of the midlife crisis, although he never used this exact term. Jung's own personal experience at midlife led him to see and appreciate the pain and potential of this stage of life. The sense of solitude that people are faced with at this time in life is apparent again and again—in psychotherapy, but also in fictional and non-fictional life histories. In the final chapter of this book we shall be looking at two cases of women whose midlife crisis was so deeply involved with the challenge and pain of accepting solitude that they almost missed the deeper possibilities inherent in the situation of the moment. Their real, concrete abandonment at the moment becomes so important, becomes such an acute center of attention, that the deeper aspects of the problem tend to be neglected. The fear of solitude becomes the problem instead of what is involved in it; for example, the person's deeper ambivalence about solitude, the necessity of a certain proportion of solitude and separation, fantasies of grandiosity or at least hopes for development, the deeper, existential solitude of the human being, the possibilities of new direction inherent in the new situation. When it comes to the question of solitude, people tend to get trapped in the witch's clutches. Why? Because the deep and actually appropriate introversion of this stage in life in no way corresponds to the image of what people generally feel is "normal."

As we have seen, it is actually with each step in its development, with each progressive maturation of the personality, and with each new and, therefore, daring situation that a child leaves a position of security for new, virgin land. In this same manner, solitude is an unavoidable step on the way to every further development. And, thus, it accompanies the life of the adult; every time a person dares to speak out, voicing his or her own opinion, however unpopular it may be, he or she is daring to take a step into solitude. The fears involved are of being denigrated, punished, excluded from, or ridiculed by the group. The heroic stance is a difficult one to take, even for those who have felt supported in early life. The education to moral courage, a social and human ideal too rarely fostered in our times, is a matter of conscious education, and not of haphazard education to conformity. That the individual tends to say nothing rather than daring to speak his or her mind is a fact of life which was noted already in the first century of this era by the Roman historian Tacitus (55-115): "He who is silent, voices his assent." The silent majority of 20th-century fame is obviously not a new phenomenon, but one which makes us painfully aware of how very difficult it is for us as human beings to assume our own solitude. Opting for solitude in the face of injustice, and for the sake of higher ideals, is a deeply human challenge. The stage is set for the capacity to do so very early on in life when the capacity to be alone is or is not fostered.

THE NECESSITY OF SOLITUDE
❧

Before leaving the topic of the search for solitude I need to say a word or two of the plain necessity of solitude. I am not thinking here of such extremes as Nietzsche, who rejoiced in what he called his "homeland of solitude" (in *Zarathustra*).[28] I am thinking rather of normal, day-to-day solitude, like that of the *paterfamilias* in the 18th-century Chinese tapestry (see page 128). As the title tells us, here we have a man out for a walk with his dog on a Sunday afternoon. We know that in Japan, the most overpopulated country in the world (with more people per square mile than any other), individual people have very little privacy. But it is exactly here in Japan that the tradition of small, quiet gardens set aside for solitary moments and meditation is still strong and important today. A certain amount of solitude is necessary for people to feel all right. And most likely the amount of solitude necessary varies from era to era, from culture to culture. Creative work evidently requires solitude. The ivory tower of the Romantic poets, and the garret of the poor poet refer to a reality of which Graham Greene spoke in his final years. In a B.B.C.

---

28. Friedrich Nietzsche, *Thus Spake Zarathustra*, Thomas Common, translator (New York: Random, 1982) or Walter Kaufmann, translator (New York & London, Penguin, 1978).

Figure 12. A man out for a walk with his dog. Chinese tapestry, 18th century. Vienna: Österreichisches Museum für Angewandte Kunst.

interview, Greene spoke of the pains, but also of the necessity, of solitude: although he found it personally hard, he knew that he needed to be alone to be able to write. One of the most common and socially acceptable forms of the search for solitude today is the vacation. During this time we are allowed to retreat from our habitual surroundings and duties for a certain, relatively short space of time. We seek replenishment in the company of those closest to us, or we are completely alone in a more or less isolated place, be it nature or another city in which we know no one or few people. This is the type of reposeful break from the stress of daily life which we see in the Chinese woodcut.

Such little islands of repose during a busy day, a busy week or during the year are restful, replenishing, vitalizing. Perhaps this is the key behind the regenerative qualities of sleep: sleep is actually a complete withdrawal from the world, and getting one's sleep means setting apart and even scheduling a specific time and place for uninterrupted solitude. The private space necessary for a human being, the solitary moments which refresh, is a completely different feeling tone than either of those we have been talking of in these first two chapters. In the first chapter the tone was rather one of desperation at being "alone and abandoned"; in this chapter, there was more a sense of elation at daring to seek solitude like God. Here we have a more natural need of solitude, a need that is felt and demanded by the body. Perhaps even certain illnesses, or maybe all, in a certain way, are a way the body demands a certain proportion of seclusion, respite from the world of culture and civilization, of socializing.

But, let us once again pose the question: are fantasies of grandeur always lurking in the aspiration to solitary retreat? Is one always seeking to be "above it all" when one withdraws from the crowd? On an inner psychic level, solitude is always associated with hopes or yearning for something better. As I have said, creative processes require a certain proportion of solitude. We can call it a period of introversion or incubation. Each of these terms indicates a moment in which one is thrown back onto oneself, with nobody else to rely upon. The focus is inward and, therefore, the world outside—society—is of less import. This is the moment in which we are faced with our own personal destiny.

However normal the search for solitude may be—as an integrated aspect of the systolic and diastolic movements of life, toward and away from others—there is, I believe, always in the search for solitude a moment of elation, superiority, a search for something better, higher. In the search for society, relationships, and congeniality, we are seeking contact and warmth, a feeling of being held by warm, human, caring relationships. In the search for solitude we are looking for something that is lacking in this type of experience—a depth of involvement in oneself, contact with other values, often spiritual ones, not infrequently, a heightened sense of one's self. And this, too, must be considered as normal.

CHAPTER THREE

Psychotherapy

The Bittersweet Reality of Solitude

The first part of this chapter is devoted to the psychotherapeutic treatment of solitude, or rather to how the question of solitude in psychotherapeutic treatment focuses on the central ambivalence or polyvalence about solitude. In fact all of what we have seen in the first two polarized chapters is actually to be found on some level in normal people suffering from or rejoicing in solitude. This is actually the truth of the matter most of the time, but this is exactly the most difficult point to establish. When I think of my patients and what they say about their experience of solitude, most complain bitterly of feeling alone or misunderstood and isolated, even alienated from others; some also yearn to be on their own, to flee the obligations they feel unavoidable; some seek a "high" in solitary experiences, and others just enjoy being alone sometimes. Few and far between are those who can find within themselves and then express more than one of these feeling states in connection to solitude.

Depressive clients reveal most clearly but nevertheless unconsciously their ambivalence about solitude: consciously they suffer from feeling different, apart, isolated from others. Their sense is that they are not understood, that no one really understands them and that they are often being insulted, denigrated, rejected. This is a major complaint. On the other hand, they seem to flee into solitude. Ashamed of being rejected, they feel unworthy of human contact and isolate themselves further still. They lose their emotional attachment to the world.[1] Negative images of themselves predominate consciousness; buried very deep in the unconscious are hopes and feelings that they are very special: they are actually unappreciated by the world.

One of the very earliest accounts of a case of depression is Homer's description of Bellerophon: here the polyvalences of solitude are quite evident. Bellerophon, who tried to reach the home of the gods on Mount Olympus on the back of the winged horse, Pegasus, is well known. That he failed in his ambitious plans and plunged into the Aegean Sea we all have heard, but his further punishment by the gods is less well known. Homer reports:

> Bellerophon was hated by all the gods.
> Across the Alean plain he wandered, all alone,
> Eating his heart out, a fugitive on the run
> from the beaten tracks of men.[2]

The fact that he "ate his heart out" shows how much Bellerophon suffered from his rejection by the gods. But Homer is significantly unclear on the question of whether Bellerophon fled the society of men *because* he was rejected by the gods, i.e., if he retreated because he was ashamed of this punishment, or if this *was* his punishment: to be exiled from the society of men, too. He both retreated and was rejected, or was rejected and then retreated. People today often react to feeling rejected by withdrawing further still. We have seen such reactions in Petrarch, Rousseau, and Thoreau, too. But these poets seem to have rejoiced in their solitude: especially Thoreau and Petrarch seem to have idealized their solitary stance and its joys: the rejection and suffering seems to have been more denied. It is very difficult to allow both feeling states to exist. People can seemingly suffer from their alienation from others and yet still unconsciously be seeking it. Before we leave Bellerophon, let us note that Bellerophon's act was considered one of *hubris*, unmeasured pride,

1. Aaron T. Beck, John A. Rush, and Gary Emery, *Cognitive Therapy of Depression* (New York: Guilford Press, 1987).
2. Homer. *The Iliad*, Robert Fagles, trans. (London: Penguin, 1990), l.200 ff.

and was punished as such by the gods. Isolating himself from the society of men, setting himself apart from them and reaching for something so much higher, for the heights of the gods on Mount Olympus, was an act punished by isolation. The ambitiousness of his act set Bellerophon apart from human society. This was then also a punishment. People tend to withdraw into solitude when their pride is hurt, when they feel disappointed in themselves, in the way others see them, or in their relationships to others.

The bittersweet reality of solitude? Yes. Our attitude toward solitude is basically paradoxical, but most of our honest feelings involve deeply paradoxical, seemingly irreconcilable opposite states: love and hate both belong to our feelings toward "loved ones," cowardice and bravery battle within us in situations demanding moral courage; disgust and fascination rule our hearts and minds when we are confronted with catastrophe. This is certainly normal for human beings, although we often have difficulty accepting such a complex emotional reality. William Willeford coined the term "complex feeling judgments" to describe such reactions.[3] One major goal of therapy is to help us learn to become aware of and to tolerate the polyvalences in our feelings, to allow room for the normal chaos belonging to the daily life of emotions. Becoming aware, for example, of the fact that we not only are suffering terribly from being alone, but also that we isolate ourselves further still is essential for any realistic judgment of ourselves and our situation. No new adjustments can be made if we do not appreciate these divergent and less congruent aspects of our reality.

A woman I shall call Kathy came to see me because she was feeling terribly irrational pangs of jealousy. She felt left out, abandoned, and rejected by her boyfriend, especially when other women were mentioned. The other women did not even need to be present. He just had to mention a woman, even one he had known years ago, and it was enough to set off excruciating flames of jealousy. Jealousy is one of those very shameful emotions which isolate people: they feel alone and misunderstood in this kind of passion and

3. William Willeford, *The Fool and his Sceptre: A Study of Clowns, Jesters & Their Audience* (Evanston, IL: Northwestern University Press, 1969), p. x.

then they isolate themselves further still. No one can understand, but actually the person finds little understanding within for such an unacceptable emotion. When, with time, Kathy realized that I could understand and accept her jealousy as a valid part of her, the major topic of interest shifted to a more generalized feeling of being left out. Actually, as we were to discover together, it was Kathy who retreated whenever she felt hurt. Whenever she felt, for example, that her boyfriend did not justly appreciate her, she would decide that it was just the time when she needed to write a letter home, to clean her apartment, to go shopping, swimming, jogging, or dancing—alone. The history of her feeling left out and of her retreating to do something really important is long; it shows a pattern of quasi-automatic reactions to being left out. For, as one of five children and the only girl, Kathy really often did find herself left out: the boys did not want to be bothered with their little sister. Kathy's Mom was very preoccupied with trying to keep her Dad happy. A very dissatisfied man, he was often complaining, yelling, or screaming about something. From this initial situation, Kathy learned a few basic things which she unconsciously followed for many years in her adult life. She learned to write whenever she felt left out. Her Mom had even suggested on several occasions then, "Why don't you write a story?" when Kathy was feeling bored at home alone. And she learned that to get attention you have to excel, to do a lot of sports, to swim very far, to jog regularly and well. Kathy became involved in two directions—writing and sports. In both, excellence was a major point. She needed to be alone and she needed to be very good and special, i.e., a lonely heroine-type. Kathy retreated into solitude in order to achieve the same kind of "solitary" position as a diamond, alone because she was someone very special. The sad part of this goal was that it was not at all what she wanted and needed. She actually yearned for deep attachments, probably even symbiotic fusion with the world, and she really felt lonely, left out, and unappreciated. Her sense of self-esteem was very unstable.

One important aspect of therapy was Kathy's discovery of her feelings about being left out; she found a lot of anger there. These very essential feelings had sort of been skipped over. And now, in its place were such immense aggressions that she repeatedly had night- and day-dreams of frightfully cruel and aggressive scenes. She came to realize this during a vacation in a very peaceful foreign country. Going for a walk through a rural area, she saw in her mind's eye the local farmers, lurking behind the crests of the mountains with machine guns, all aimed at her and ready to fire. This image was so clear and so ridiculous to her that she came home quite jolted and with the question: "What is all of this about?" This is how we were finally able to discuss Kathy's long repressed aggression, and its sources in feeling neglected and unappreciated. Needless to say, this kind of vision then stopped plaguing her: the tone of her dreams and fantasies changed at this point. Kathy started to dream more about love and her romantic needs.

Kathy both retreated into solitude and feared it. Helping her to become aware of this basic ambivalence was not simple. She was much less aware of her retreat into solitude than she was of her feeling abandoned. She withdrew in a very refined and nuanced manner. Not only did she announce now and then that she absolutely had to go home to read or write, she also retreated during her normal, day-to-day interactions with other people. This behavior pattern, or pattern of non-communication, became a subject of great concern during therapy for the very simple reason that again and again I found myself falling asleep during our sessions. One day I felt that I simply had to tell her that I was having trouble staying awake. I had hesitated saying anything about it, fearing that she would be terribly insulted. She was, in fact, hurt by my words, but she was also glad to have her own observations confirmed. She had noticed me struggling to keep my eyes open. She was also glad to have the opportunity to discuss a topic she had suspected about herself for a long time: she actually felt that she put up an inner fence—she called it a buffer—between herself and the world. Afraid of being hurt by others, she tried not to let them get too close: she shielded herself when she was with other people by talking in a superficial, impersonal manner, not ever really expressing her true opinions. "The buffer phenomenon" became a very important topic. And Kathy began to become sensitive to the moments when she felt she needed the buffer. She learned to ask herself if she really wanted to protect herself so much. Consequently, Kathy less often felt left out, for she was allowing others to get close to her. As a consequence, Kathy definitely felt less alone and abandoned ; she slowly learned to relate in a more personal way both to herself and to others. Essential in this new adaptation was my letting her know that she had been putting me to sleep—i.e., shutting me out and isolating herself from any real contact with me or with herself.

A ROOM OF ONE'S OWN

❧

We exist as social beings. And so, cut off from others, we would be living in an acoustic and an emotional vacuum. We are missing our all-important echo, our projection screen, an object for our fantasies and our emotions, our tenderness and our empathy. Our capacities for both self-perception and for adequate perception of the realities of the world is severely limited when the dialogue with the other(s) is lacking. Gretel can only learn to see the real limitations of the duck's strength when she has come to inhabit a room of her own. Before this all important experience, the world is either a gingerbread house or a cruel mother: there is nothing in between. Cinderella is either a sad and lonely dejected cindermaid or a glorious and flirtatious princess decked out in silver and gold before she can mature into a potential wife and partner for the prince. As long as she is isolated from others, she cannot see herself in a realistic light. Her lack of any real communication with the outer world reflects her lack of any real communication with her inner world. In such a situation she cannot see herself in a realistic light. And her lack of confidence in herself is compensated by the grandiose fantasies of superiority which she cultivates in private. This is actually the only communication going on between Cinderella and her images of her superior self. But everyone consists of more than these secret images of excellence. It is only in coming to discover and inhabit a room of our own that we can become people interested in others.

"A room of one's own," is the way Virginia Woolf described what a woman needs in order to be able to write.[4] She explained this as a space in which a woman can be on her own, without continuous interruptions. At the same time, this is a room in a house that is inhabited by others, so that the woman is not completely cut off from the world, from her own, personal world. Not a solitary retreat as in a cloister or a desert, but a *living space* in which a certain degree of privacy is granted—this is a room of one's own. Within such a space, according to Virginia Woolf, a woman can develop her creative abilities: the solitude she is allowed to enjoy here enables her to get in touch with herself. This implies that communication is the ultimate goal of the spatial separation, communication with the world within herself and with a world without— the potential reader of the writing. As the room is not isolated, but is rather within the bounds of a house, the woman's house (that is, it is a room, a space that is annexed or in close connection to her own, personal world), she remains in contact with her own world: it is within a tangible distance. She can cultivate the fantasy of getting in touch with it whenever she feels the need to do so. And so, this is not an enforced, but a chosen solitude, and it is at the same time necessarily relative, allowing for nuances, for change, for flexibility.

I know no better image for describing the kind of inner, psychic space and situation necessary for the development of a mature and satisfied personality, or, as I have put it earlier on here, necessary for the creative act of development. The capacity for being alone and at the same time for remaining in contact with others is, I believe, a goal and, at the same time, a prerequisite, not only for all creative but also for all developmental processes.

C. G. Jung has often been misunderstood on this point. He spoke of individuation as a goal of psychic development, of allowing the unique individual personality to unfold. Although he often

---

4. Virginia Woolf, *A Room of One's Own*, 1929 (London & New York: Granada, 1981).

cautioned against collective values, he by no means devaluated the importance of commitment to the collective, to society. In fact, in one of the sentences which I find the most revealing on this point, he said, "Individuation is impossible without a relationship to one's environment."[5]

I would go so far as to say that the development of the capacity to assume one's existential solitude and, at the same time, to open up and to remain in dialogue with oneself and with the world well describes the goal of any psychotherapy. In terms of a room of one's own, this means that a need to find and furnish "a room of one's own" is the ideal goal of any psychotherapeutic endeavor. This chapter is devoted to the elaboration of the applicability of this symbolic image to human development. In it we shall delve into the theory and practice of psychotherapy through the elaboration of case examples. Implicit and basic to the image is, of course, the capacity for being alone. What it means to be alone, how this capacity seems to be developed through satisfactory early experiences, and examples of people who suffered because of their lack of this capacity will be of central interest here.

On a purely practical level it is very interesting to point out the importance that a room of one's own develops in concrete reality during the course of psychotherapy. Again and again I have seen that people in psychotherapy come to feel the need for having such a room, for concretizing this image. They suddenly feel an urge to re-arrange or refurnish their own room, the space they feel the most connected to: they seem to find a more personal connection to a certain living space, and come to identify with it more consciously. For example, they find they absolutely need an easy chair in the room, as a place to sit comfortably and read. Or they feel they need a lounge there to lie down if they feel like it. This means that they come to realize and take seriously their own needs, and are trying to adapt their lives and living conditions to accommodate these needs as much as the present reality permits. Sometimes they even need to find new living conditions which can better allow them to accommodate their real, serious needs. Often these needs have to

5. C. G. Jung, *Aion*, Collected Works, Vol. 9. II, §257.

do with more room to withdraw and be on their own. The drive for filling this new space in a creative manner comes to express itself in actions and words, as more personally motivated solutions to daily problems are sought: decisions and communication, relationships, too, become more personally determined, more individually colored. This is by no means to say that people in psychotherapy become unadapted to their surroundings. Rather their adaptations are made more consciously and are less prompted by an unconscious need to conform. Actually people seem to develop both an increased need and increased capacity for becoming involved in meaningful relationships.

The development of the need for a room of one's own is interesting. It is generally preceded by a period of retreat, a time of withdrawal and solitude. We might even better call it a time of incubation, when the person turns inward, concentrating his or her energies on the inner developmental processes. This gives the strength and certitude which allows for re-orientation. It allows for the time and space necessary for one to reflect on oneself and the situation at hand and, thus, to find a suitable re-orientation. Within the psychotherapeutic setting this is not a phase of incommunicability. Rather the communication is turned inward in a new type of attention to and dialogue with inner processes.

The psychotherapist is a partner in communication and a guide in encouraging the contact with the inner world. Here the attention becomes focused on dreams and fantasies, memories, thoughts, feelings, physical sensations, and even pain, all of which are often just barely perceived, heard as mere whisperings. Affective states are of great import, for whatever moves us in our relationships with the world and with ourselves is a powerful agent. Reactivating the contact with this untiring stream of being is of the essence. It is also, naturally, one way in which the capacity for being alone is fostered.

By way of example, I can mention the case of Mickey whom I spoke of in the preceding chapter. One of his main complaints at the beginning of therapy was a fear of separation, of being abandoned whenever he did or said what he really felt. He also often complained of not feeling understood by his family and close

At such times he would retreat emotionally and even some- physically. On the one hand, Mickey feared solitude, on the r, he sought it. This is the depressive and wounded retreat we have been talking about.

In Mickey's case the theme of solitude is a red thread: it not only runs clearly and strongly in a negative fashion through his present life, it has also determined his development in the past: he has acted it out and it also becomes a positive guiding image in the work. We have already seen how, as an adolescent, Mickey tried the ascetic retreat in the form of *anorexia nervosa*. This is a painful chapter for him to speak of now, but I believe it to have been a decisive one for his development. Having grown up in a very conflictual family situation, Mickey knew only a mother who constantly threatened to abandon the family, even to kill herself, if she did not get the love, admiration, and cooperation she needed. His parents fought a lot and most fights ended with dramatic threats on the part of his mother. One essential reason why these threats were so impressive and so frightening is, of course, Mickey's father. He was most often not at home and was quite weak and ineffectual when he *was* there. No counterbalance, no opposingly strong position was offered by the paternal side. And so we see the classical case of a child that really had no choice but the orientation to this one unstable parental figure.

It is no wonder that Mickey learned to keep any personal feelings and opinions to himself and had difficulty even realizing what was good for him. Of primary importance, from his point of view, was keeping his mother alive and happy: he felt that he could do this by living and breathing agreement with her. His anorectic retreat into the family attic was an extreme and relatively unconscious attempt to free himself from this Siamese-twin situation with his mother and her opinions; his deeper and unconscious goal was to free himself to become an adult. As I mentioned in the previous chapter, Mickey was also trying desperately to find another orientation than merely the maternal one. In eating little he was imitating his father who was dieting at the time and, in this way, looking to this other parental model for orientation. The seclusion of his retreat also permitted another contact with himself, and especially to other, very secret but also very necessary private aspects of his being: the grandiose self images which I believe everyone—and especially teenagers—need to have and to cultivate in order to grow.

Given the severity of *anorexia nervosa*, an illness so well known today, I must repeat here that it must be seen, in this case, as in most others, from the perspective of a young person attempting to become an individual, to extricate him or herself from a family situation that impedes freedom of development. In Mickey's specific case, he was a very unstable attached child, living in constant fear of abandonment as a punishment for individualism, or even individuation. Had he not developed this symptom he most likely would have remained overly attached to this unstable object in an even more severe and pathological manner.

Paradoxically enough, one of the most powerful positive images to develop early on in therapy was that of a cave. It came up spontaneously in one of our initial hours as a place in which Mickey felt comfortable, where he was on his own, where he could invite friends to be with him, but could also just as well be alone. From Mickey's perspective this is a rather spectacular image of individuation, echoing quite exactly what I mean by "a room of one's own." The image was born in a session during which he was complaining of his fear of separation, more concretely, of his fears that his wife would leave him if he were not quite so understanding toward her. We had no trouble tracing these fears back to his relationship with his mother, where Mickey was always on the spot, always over-ready to adapt to her whims, lest she go off in a huff, disappointed in her son and even kill herself. But the redeeming character of the cave, in itself a mother symbol, is important. If Mickey can find a space of his own in which he feels comfortable, then he can feel at home in himself; we can say that he can integrate maternal comfort, feel rooted in himself and in contact with his own vitality. Then and only then can he be alone without feeling abandoned. A room of his own is just another way of describing this cave image.

THE CAPACITY FOR BEING ALONE

⮐

The capacity for being alone depends on the existence and reliability of the contact with the inner world and its images—its centers of energy. People who can be alone with themselves are inevitably people who cultivate a relationship with themselves and with these intimate elements of the personality. I spoke in the second chapter of the importance of strong inner images, reliable emotional ties that provide a sense of positive and constant companionship, no matter what the outer situation is like. Psychotherapy attempts to cultivate this type of contact with the inner world. The model on which it is based bares striking resemblances with the very early life experiences described by Donald W. Winnicott as essential for developing the capacity for being alone.

Winnicott,[6] the rightfully renowned pediatrician turned psychoanalyst, again and again took up the topic of solitude, considering it an important aspect in the life of every human being. In one such instance he developed the idea of the importance for the small infant of "being alone in the presence of another." In such moments of accompanied solitude, he said, the child has the time and space necessary for sensing out its own impulses and following up on them. Under such ideal conditions, Winnicott felt, the infant can explore itself, it can sense things going on inside itself. Essential in the experience is that the child is allowed to be in contact with its own sphere of being without the interference of another person, and yet in the company of another. The quality of this presence of the other is the critical point: it must be felt, palpable and at the same time not intrusive. This means that no demands be made, no expectations expressed, not even well-meaning interventions, like suggestions of how the child could do its self-appointed task in a better way. (I believe that it is in this context that one can under-

---

6. Donald Winnicott, "Die Fähigkeit zum Alleinsein" [The Capacity to be Alone] in *International Journal of Psychoanalysis*, 1958, pp. 416-420.

stand how much little children express the need to have a parent with them at bedtime, even to have a parent lie down with them then. With this comforting, silent presence the child can allow itself to drift off into its own, very private world, to fall sleep. Instead of the terror lurking in the emptiness of sleep, there can be an atmosphere of warmth and security of going off into new and undiscovered regions within oneself: letting go can become an experience that feels good, instead of one fraught with fear.) Winnicott stated unequivocally that this type of experience provides the foundations necessary for a mature person's capacity for being alone. With the imprint of such an experience, one can not feel too direly alone, for this reliable and positive inner image or presence holds or anchors the person within him- or herself and within the world. Although Winnicott did not state this explicitly, this other who is present, but silent, is obviously an empathic other, approving all the while, palpable but not making him- or herself all too invasively felt. Under such conditions a person can feel secure enough to be able to be alone.

In psychotherapy a similar situation is constellated. The therapy arrangement provides the space and time for a person to get involved with him- or herself and with the inner world. Not infrequently, no words are spoken: silence is an important aspect belonging to therapy. It provides the space necessary for delving into one's depths. The presence of the therapist is a given; his or her abstinence can be understood as a kind of holding without making demands: it provides a freedom to discover feelings and impulses, and to follow up on them, to become involved with them. The ultimate goal of cultivating this private space is, as in the infant, the creation and cultivation of the capacity for being alone and yet not feeling alone. As with the care-taker in infancy who was there without being intrusive, the analyst is there, an encouraging and empathic figure of support who is eminently reliable. He or she is like the doorman to the inner world; thanks to this presence a person can dare to get in touch with, to open up the communication with the inner world. The contact with the inner world, with the life, images, energy, and the interest present there, is the ultimate goal of any work in psychotherapy. This goal cannot be achieved without the security of the other's presence; being alone in the presence of another who holds and makes no demands is a basic prerequisite for any healthy development.

THE IMPOSSIBILITY OF BEING ALONE

～

Perhaps the best way of showing how important it is for a person to have known the experience of being alone in the presence of another is to show what can happen when this is not the case. John first comes to mind here, a young man who said that as far as he could remember he was never ever really allowed to be alone. He had to enlist in the army in order to escape from his over-protective mother. And so, it was quite understandable that he declared from time to time and with a great deal of affect, "I would just like to get away from it all, leave everything and live alone. (pause) I love solitude!" What this young man was actually yearning for in his fervent statement became evident in one of our early hours. He came in distraught, for he felt an uncomfortable pressure in his chest. It was just frustrating to have this symptom again: he had already started therapy and was learning so much about himself. I decided to try to help John try to find out what this pressure was all about. I do not want to go into a long account of the way in which we approached this physical symptom, turning up its volume and getting involved in its language. I have given a detailed description of this kind of work in my book on chaos.[7] Just briefly I will say that by paying close and detailed attention to the pressure, John became aware of many aspects of his physical sensations and ultimately was led to a fantasy image that he felt prompted to draw. (See page 148.)

John had begun psychotherapeutic treatment exactly because of the anxieties which he felt in the form of contractions in his chest. He described his symptoms in the following way: "It feels

---

7. *Chaos & Order in the World of the Psyche* (London: Routledge, 1992).

like a heavy weight is on my chest. I feel nervous. An urge comes over me to bite my nails: I don't want to do it, but I have to." John was fortunate in his attitude to these symptoms: he was convinced they were symptoms, signs pointing to something else of which he was not aware. He neither rejected nor ignored them; he had them checked by his medical doctor and when he found out that there was nothing physically wrong, he decided to try psychotherapy. This is, in itself, a very healthy attitude to a physical disorder: too many people today tend to take physical reactions as a reality which speaks only of the body's suffering. Most frequently it is the psyche, or let us say, the person as a whole who is suffering. The body makes itself heard and felt, but the psyche's other means of communication—fear, depression, anger and insecurity—are too threatening to be admitted.

John was the second of two children born to a family who lived in a small town. He did not really like his brother, never did, but as children they never fought. As adults they never argued, but they did not have very much to do with each other: John especially tended to avoid contact with his brother. John left home when he was 20 and only managed to do so by volunteering for service in the army. Now he lived in a big city and seldom went home to see his family. He felt quite guilty about this, but somehow he just could not. Whenever he had to be there he felt extremely uncomfortable.

Let us first listen to John's comments on his picture and what he was trying to show in it; later I shall go into my understanding of what lay behind John's fantasies. The monumental presence looming over the little stick figure is meant to be his mother. As the young man clearly remembered, and now he was 30, his mother had never left him alone: she was always there for him and never let him be alone, either. Her presence was always a given and it made itself felt in many ways. She always tried to be extremely helpful. Even to this day she was like this. If he told her he planned to go to Jamaica on holiday, for example, she would be sending him brochures, maps, travel accounts, as well as practical hints (on Jamaica, the tropics, traveling in general), which she gleaned from talking to countless people about his plans. Her main concern in life

Figure 13. John's fantasy image. Used by permission.

seems to have been sweeping away any difficulties her children might encounter, protecting them from all hardships and paving their way for a comfortable life. When John was 9 he broke his leg and could not go to school for awhile. His mother went to school for him, for otherwise he might miss too much. She wanted to be sure that he knew exactly what had been taught each day and had the right homework. This is but one of the many memories John told while trying to explain to me how the all-pervading maternal presence had been so oppressive to him. But it made him very upset to say this, for she really only meant this well. She was being helpful, was sacrificing herself for him. Talking of these experiences and memories, these forbidden and despicable feelings that plagued him, made him feel terribly guilty toward his well-meaning mother, but it nevertheless gave him a sense of relief.

A more detailed look at John's drawing is necessary in order to understand what lay behind all of this; the connection between his suffering and the topic of solitude then becomes apparent. John intended to show here what kind of pressure he had been exposed to daily as a child. He would sit down in his room to do his schoolwork and his mother would nag at him constantly to do his work; he would refuse, wanting to go out to play instead. She would lock him in his room and force him to stay there until he finished his work. He could not concentrate then and felt only the pressure of "having" to do something he did not want to do. But he could not do anything else. He would sit there, getting all confused, in a daze. It felt as if his mother were trying to conduct him, to force him to dance to her music: it felt to him as if she were constantly looming over him, repeating again and again the same theme, that he had to go on, do his school work, learn, study, learn, study. During the course of therapy, John came to understand the pressure which came from both his parents, although his mother had been the main executor: the father had little education and was a roofer who worked hard and long hours, but he finally did very well for himself and his family. He had always hoped that his son would have an easier time in life, and felt this could be attained by enabling him to get a better education. Of course, this meant that John had to do well in school. This was, unfortunately, not the case.

Now, what impression do we get when we look at John's drawing? What we see here looks like a unit, not a domineering mother and her poor, helpless child. John and his mother fit together like pieces of a machine that belong together, like a wheel fitting into cogs. This is most apparent in the squiggles that are meant to be his mother's hair: they are at the same time the confusion over John's head. What grows from her head, her hair, are symbolically ideas that become John's own ideas. Interesting is the lack of space in the picture—there is no space between John and his mother: not only his head, but even the feet of his chair and even his table touch the mother or are touched by her. There is no escaping: there is no free room, no private space, and this is the bottom line of John's basic problem. Interesting is the similarity in the arms: both John and his mother have arms stretched out in a gesture of helplessness. John's helplessness he was quite aware of. His mother's was less immediately apparent to him: she had the tools necessary to conduct him: she was the leader, there was no doubt of that, but, nevertheless, she was actually also helpless. She put pressure on him, tried to persuade him of the importance of learning, even had the power of locking him in his room and not letting him go out to play until he finished his homework. And yet, in the long run, she was also absolutely powerless. In reality this had also been the case, for despite all of his mother's well-meant (and also personally determined) coaching, John left school before he got his diploma. One day he just gave up and refused to go back. On an inner psychic level, this image was active: it meant that John (like his mother previously) put enormous pressure on himself, but it was ineffectual. All he could do in the face of this self-imposed pressure was to try to get out, as he had done in quitting school.

The differentiation between John and his mother are important to note here. John portrays himself as a wiry stick figure, full of jags and with few curves. She, on the contrary, is a rounded, arabesque figure with anatomical parts that flow together to form a whole—head, trunk and arms. Also, the boy is really tiny in comparison with the monumental figure looming over him. These differences have a realistic side, reflecting the physical differences which always really do exist between a small child and its parents. The physical dimensions separating a child from its parents is a perspective that Kafka described dramatically in his *Letter to His Father*.[8] It is something which we, as parents, should try to keep in mind, for it means that our actions and words, even our gestures and facial expressions, are naturally very much magnified for our children. This is one reason why these parental relationships are of such importance: the extraordinarily unequal division of power makes for a situation in which an immensely impressive being holds the fate of a tiny fly in its hands. John's drawing is not a comforting image of the feeling of security of a little child in the arms of a strong and reliable person. It is rather a threatening image, full of

---

8. Franz Kafka, *Letter to His Father* (New York: Schocken, 1987).

feelings of impending danger. This impression of John's relationship to his mother, especially, is confirmed in a terrifying fantasy which John had repeatedly as a child. He would lie in bed at night and suddenly the walls of his room would begin to close in on him. They would get closer and closer until they practically squeezed him into nothingness. Here we have a concretization of what actually did go on: there were no boundaries, no limits between him and his mother. She was everywhere and was always getting closer and closer, not leaving him any space to develop. Theirs was a symbiotic connection which threatened to smother the child. The little boy would try to wake up from this waking fantasy: he would pinch himself, get up out of bed, touching the walls. He did this again and again, trying to get the walls to move back to where they belonged, but they just continued closing in on him. Finally at some point they retreated and he would fall asleep. But the fantasy would turn up again and again, one night after the other.

We have here the opposite of "being alone in the presence of another." The nocturnal fantasy and the picture both show how a constant and demanding maternal presence, but also a helpful presence, precludes all possibilities of ever really being alone. This also meant that discovering himself and maturing into an independent person was almost impossible, for John was never left alone, neither physically nor psychologically. He was allowed no private space in which he might get in touch with himself, to get to know his own personality traits, his own specific, personal needs, his likes and dislikes, his impulses. His mother was omnipresent and intrusive, even to the point of going to school for him, entering into a realm that was so obviously his and his alone. But it was all well meant, and this made it harder yet for the boy.

One result of his not having been allowed to experience "being alone in the presence of another" was John's need as an adult to get away from others. He needed this in order to avoid the pressures that he fantasized coming from others. When friends would ask him to come along for a night out, their offer was more of a demand than an offer. He had to refuse and retreat, to withdraw and do his own thing. Being alone was the only way John could imagine being himself and not having the feeling that others were trying to influence him. But, as he came to find, John also lived under extreme pressures when nobody was around. This was an essential realization. He pushed himself—to learn more, to read more, to ride more miles on his bicycle. He had internalized the pressure of this monumental maternal figure to the extent that she was inside him; as often as he could, he projected it, and the pressure that came from it, onto the outer world. That made things easier: he could go into the opposition and ignore his own difficulties with himself. Of course, this inner figure was never satisfied with him, so John cherished fantasies of not needing anyone, and through this solitary stance he became the hero—fantasies of grandeur. From the poor student, suffering from feeling stupid, he became in his very private fantasy world a great man who needed no one, who read more than others, who walked more, who rode more. Any subject was convenient for making him a hero. And being alone was an essential part of his heroism. He needed no one, and, therefore, he was a hero.

In psychotherapy it was important for John to be able to make quite different experiences. The little boy who never confided in anyone for fear of getting too close, fearing that others would make demands on him, or overpower him, became the man who was able to confide and to grow. The hours which took place twice a week over a period of four years became precious to him, as he often said. He had not known that he could talk to anyone of these things. He was again and again surprised at the wealth of memories and fantasies slumbering in him. This is not to say that John did not go into the opposition in therapy: he did, and it was important that he allow himself to do so, for his need to conform to the powerful therapist was also a pressing one. When he ultimately decided he had had enough therapy, his declaration came like a declaration of independence, shot from a gun, with a great deal of aggressivity and little compassion. This type of refusal of care, of rejection of the figure who was responsible for furthering his maturational process was just the type of rejection he had never dared express toward his mother, or his father, for that matter. It was essential that in this penultimate moment of psychotherapy John be allowed to experience his own self-liberation. He felt it as exhilarating and was proud of himself. In his final reflections on the process he had been in during these four years, John came to realize that his liberation was one major aspect of his development which he had not been allowed to live out at home.

John's story illustrates one path on the way to finding a "room of one's own." At the end of therapy he no longer lived in, nor yearned for, a solitary retreat. He had found a room of his own in which he felt comfortable. He explored it and enjoyed its particularities, all the while remaining in contact with the real world. The threatening omnipresence of family pressures to succeed, which had loomed over him and had continued in various forms in his contacts with the world at large, was gradually replaced by a larger presence of his own which dwelt within and which felt more comfortable. The creative aspect of this room changed a great deal throughout time. From pressure to perform in accordance with expectations from others—and from himself—John became someone who required excellence and creativity of himself in many artistic works he did before and during the initial years of therapy. The creative urge, which was especially strong in him, slowly became an urge for creative solutions within the normal context of his life, his own solutions to everyday problems. The way he dealt with his conflicts, with his needs, with his daily life became more important to him. At the end of therapy, John's solutions grew out of himself and were constantly created anew, without relying on the demands or expectations of society at large, or of his own personal family and friends. The readjustment in the domain of self-worth, his own reappraisal of himself, was also an important area of change. He became increasingly aware of the grandiose fantasies of himself that he had cultivated and tried to conform to, all the while feeling that he was quite stupid and inept at making anything out of himself. This made him feel quite sad, for he realized that the fantasies flourished when he rejected himself and denigrated his own capacities. John's story is a rather typical one. Although it is certainly very personal, it is one prototype of the problem of solitude. I would call it the search for solitude in order to find oneself: the temptation of grandiosity was a necessary aspect, leading to a more realistic self-evaluation.

THE THREAT OF BEING ALONE

⌒·

The following story is also true, very personal, and yet it corresponds to a typical pattern. I call it suffering from solitude because one feels dreadfully hurt and unloved. This is the story of a woman I shall call Rita, a woman aged 50. This is a time in life when biological developments taking place within her and her new social situation force a woman to look at herself and her life in a new and more conscious way than ever before. Like any other period of transition, the menopause is necessarily difficult. If all goes well, it can be seen and appreciated, often only in retrospect, as a time of deep introversion and self-examination, a systolic movement toward solitude when solutions to a new life situation are sought.

Rita began her first psychotherapy when her three children were in their teens and were becoming more and more involved in their own worlds. She felt alone and lacking in the kind of emotional warmth her nest had provided both for her children and for herself. She came to see me five years after the children had moved out and she was feeling very dissatisfied with her life. Rita had continued to work part-time while her children were growing up. With the children gone, she continued to work the same relatively few number of hours in the hope that her husband, who was working on a reduced schedule, would have more time to spend with her. She had fantasies of doing things together again, going on vacation more often, just having time to enjoy each other's company. When she began therapy this wish remained unfulfilled.

The major topic of Rita's hours was her dissatisfaction with her husband and their relationship. This is often the major topic of concern in this phase of life, for the task of mothering has taken up so much space and time until now that women are not wholly involved with their spouses as long as the children are at home. They are so occupied and fulfilled by their task as mothers that they come to neglect the question of their marital relationship. Their husbands, too, may have been so involved in helping take care of the children that the relationship has not been of central concern. When the children leave home, and this generally coincides with the change of life, the marital relationship often becomes more important for the woman. The satisfaction or dissatisfaction with the marital relationship becomes a central focus. It was at this point that Rita came to realize and suffer from feeling abandoned by her husband. She was full of resentment toward him—resentment at the way he neglected the family and the fact that she had been shouldered with the task of the children so completely. He had been away from home often, and when he had been present, he had not helped her with discipline or giving the children guidelines. Rita was full of bitterness toward her husband.

After about a year of therapy she made a drawing (figure 14, page 156) during one of our sessions. It was an effort to explain how empty her living room at home felt to her. There was a corner for eating and one for sitting and talking. But this did not feel quite right to her: the colors and the arrangement of the furniture somehow did not suit her. Rita did not particularly notice at this time that there was a huge and very central lack in the middle of the room. Here there was no center of communication, no movement, no center of interest. This lack well reflected Rita's actual problem. It was not of recent date, but had been an integral part of her since early times: a center of energy was missing, one might say a feeling of being centered in herself. What Rita came to remember was times of being alone, not feeling held and comforted, and then running away from home and seeking solace with other children's families. As much as one can reconstruct such things, it seems that Rita had been "left alone in the *absence* of another." From what I came to understand of her family, her mother seems to have been extremely egocentric and her father disinterested. People were hired to take care of the children (there had been four of them). What was quite evident was the achievement orientation of the woman Rita, and of the child she had been: she had always had the impression that she had to do well in order to be seen, in order to be recognized. Even now, she felt that her parents did not appreciate her, but merely found fault with her again and again. This was the way Rita also felt about her husband—he did not appreciate her, either,

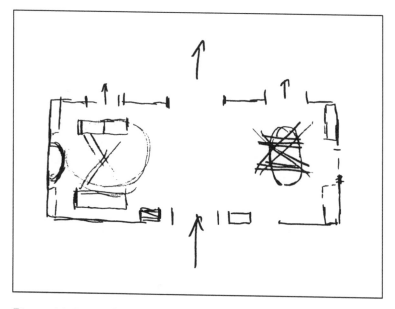

Figure 14. Rita's drawing. Used by permission.

and only found fault with her. This perception of the world and of herself tells us a great deal about Rita. She had become, as we saw with John, part of what she so consciously rejected, the demanding and unloving parent of her own inner child. She rejected herself and demanded a great deal of herself, but it was easier to see this in the world outside than as an inner psychic problem.

The lack of the "gleam in the eye of the (m)other" had formed Rita into the dissatisfied woman she had become. She felt this lack everywhere, but could not realize that it was mainly and initially in her attitude about herself that there was a major lack. Her need to feel the approving presence of another—a need that was an attempt to compensate for early lacks in this domain—made for a lot of pressure on her milieu. She had extraordinary expectations of others. And so, whenever her husband made the least innocuous remark about her, or her household, she felt very hurt, even felt destabilized. The need for his loving and supportive presence made for a great deal of pressure in the relationship. Rita's needs for praise and support from others were urgent: only with the fantasy of constant approval from her milieu could she imagine keeping a sense of her own personal value. These were obviously facts that Rita did not dare know about herself: she could, therefore, not easily acknowledge them.

A major change revealed itself after two years of therapy. It had to do with a tiny scrap of paper, torn off from the corner of an envelope, which she brought to our session. Until this time, Rita had spent the majority of her time and energy in our biweekly sessions complaining about her husband and construing all kinds of theories on what must be going on inside him in order for him to act like this or like that, at any rate, in order for him to be treating her so badly. Although I definitely considered it my task to be with her and support her, I had difficulty here, for it often seemed to me that Rita was being unjust toward her husband—misinterpreting him. This was my emotional reaction which I sometimes had to tell her point blank. It was also important for me to show Rita the pattern that repeatedly presented in our hours—of her spending her time not talking of herself, but of her husband. Her lack of interest in what was going on inside her was such a matter-of-fact reality that she could hardly realize it. One day I suggested a way we might break this pattern, a way that we might try to find out what was happening in her during those moments when her husband was being offensive toward her. I asked her to try to take note of this other, more interior perspective when one of these situations presented again. And surprisingly enough, Rita did actually come to our next hour with a ragged piece of paper on which she had quickly jotted down her feelings. The paper, its tiny size and poor quality, shows the extent to which Rita did not value, or take time for her own center of energy, for herself as a center of interest. But here, at least, she had finally tried to grasp a bit of her own inner world and that was an excellent sign. I began to gather some hope.

The words of her reflections quickly jotted on the paper expressed deep feelings of insecurity. Her husband had not shown any reaction at all one day when she had made a remark about their only daughter. He sat, reading his newspaper, hardly even looking up at her. She went off again to do her cleaning, full of terrible nagging self-doubt: "Had he heard her at all? Was he at all interested in her? Was what she had said so crazy as to justify this reaction?" She went back to him again and again, trying to talk to him, trying to get him to react. All the while she sensed how she began more and more to doubt her feelings, and even her perception of the situation. Suddenly she became angry, angry about being "abandoned." She had felt this anger toward her husband in the past, but had usually thrown something at him in such moments. This time she just let her anger be and observed, made note of it. It turned into a feeling of defiance, "No, I'm right. I see what I see and I feel what I feel and it's O.K."

In discussing this intense experience Rita gradually became aware of how dependent she was and had always been, dependent on echo, on positive, approving, even admiring reflection in another's eye. And this feeling of not getting what she needed and, therefore, of being abandoned repeatedly, almost daily, she saw now had accompanied her throughout her life. Until this point she had found satisfying systems of compensation. As a little girl she learned to achieve to gain approval; as a mother she had lived out her need for achievement with the children. Now alone with her husband, these paths, once so well known and reliable, were being denied to her. Her husband did not need her to shine; nor did he need her as the children had. He was quite capable of caring for himself—washing, ironing, and cooking. Where was Rita then to get the gleam she needed if not through her achievements? This became the central concern of our work together: how was Rita to obtain a good feeling about herself without forcing herself to achieve? It was essential for us to spend quite some time on "digesting" the dependency we had discovered. For Rita it was like coming to find she had a "hole" (as she put it) that was right in the middle of her. This hole, of course, corresponded exactly to the empty central space in the drawing she had made of her "living room." Symbolically speaking, the room in which she lived, her own inner space, was not filled out, not with a sense of who she was, nor of feelings, nothing. She was not centered in herself. Rita had lived focused on the outer world, focusing her energies on trying to please the members of her family, especially, trying to get them to rescue her from her own inner solitude.

The fact that Rita made these discoveries at age 50 may sound strange, but it is not at all so. This is the time of menopause and, as I mentioned at the beginning of Rita's story, this is the time in which women are forced, by the biological and social changes which inevitably occur, to have a deeper and longer look a themselves and their lives. Often at the menopause the basic and central problems of the personality, which have been there all along, but have not been taken care of in an appropriate manner, reappear with a tremendously demanding urgency: they need to be taken care of. Often these problems have to do with identity and self-esteem, and are like repetitions of the experiences the women had gone through in puberty, the time when similar problems are constellated. But, as we have seen in the previous chapters, puberty is also a time of the unfolding of tremendous powers. Menopause, too, is a time when women often begin to discover extremely intense energies that have been slumbering inactive in them for years. They often become very active, if they can manage to incorporate this activity within their existing social situations. When this is not possible, they tend to become impressively active and vital widows. One never would have suspected such vitality in these selfsame women before.

Rita's initial reactions to these discoveries were intense and difficult to bear. She felt absolutely distressed at discovering the hole: it seemed quite irreparable, a curse of fate. What was she to do? But things just naturally became quite different once Rita was able to see, and in part to accept, this aspect of herself as belonging to her. She began to be able to have a longer look at her hole and how it got there, how it had affected her life until now. And slowly she became more involved in herself and her own needs, spending more time in her sessions talking about herself and her inner world. She very gradually came to find a center and began to fill it out. Her living room was slowly transformed into a room of her own. Thus began a process whereby Rita began to allow her own impulses and needs to surface and to follow them. She was able to be with herself in the presence of another—me, her therapist—and to remain in contact with herself all the while. Her contacts with the world became more real and more lively, exactly because she had found a space of her own in which she did not feel lonely: she was there with all her thoughts and feelings, her likes and dislikes. And I was there in her mind, approving her existence, confirming her in the feeling that this existence of hers had a right to be, that it was justified, right, and good. The internalization of the therapist was a gradual but, as always in psychotherapy, a necessary process. I needed to become there and reliable within her, so that she could be herself, alone and yet not lonely within the world of her life, within the walls of her own home. The living room needed to become animated, vitalized, its center occupied and alive with herself and her own interests, impulses, needs, and feelings. Rita needed to be in conversation with these parts of herself in order to feel whole. This was the all important goal of our work together.

THE PEACOCK IN THE WASTELAND

❧

The following is Harry's story, a businessman in his early 40s. He sought me out because of physical symptoms that led him to consult many specialists in vain. His problem was a deep-seated sense of solitude which had come to permeate him quite completely, which made him a very unhappy man who was, nevertheless, hardly aware of his unhappiness. He just had physical problems which made him feel quite unwell and unhappy: this was his point of view. From the point of view of another aspect of his being, his development, these unpleasant and worrying physical ailments at least made Harry aware of the "way he felt" and, therefore (in an albeit impervious and perfidious way) forced him to pay attention to himself. His body's discomforts he could feel. His emotional discomfort he could not. Harry could not "feel" his emotions. From what we have seen before, we know that this means there is a lack of an inner dialogue: an empathic other on the inside is missing. Harry had no room of his own. He had not been able to be alone in the presence of another, for he had been just plain alone for most of his life, and this pattern had begun very early. Harry was born into a family that was not there for him from the very start. His parents had married, fought, and divorced when he was less than 2 years old. He never saw his father again. His mother remarried after several years, but was very taken up with her career. Her new husband was "nice," but somehow he could not fill the gap that had been left by the father. Harry spent a lot of time as a child playing with a telescope. He would look up at the skies for hours on end. What was he doing? He was looking into the skies, the heavens, the place where the age-old images of fathers belong. Symbolically speaking, we can say that he was looking for his father or a father. He did not find any.

At the same time, despite the fact that he was suffering from being alone, he was isolating himself further still. And this is a typical trait for Harry, as well as for many who suffer from inner solitude and fear abandonment: they often retreat into physical isolation from the outside world. In general, we can say that they have actually been abandoned already. What they fear has already come to pass: they have felt emotionally abandoned in relationships and retreat from the world, and also from themselves. This is the position of inner solitude we have seen again and again. The moment of retreat can, as we saw with Rita, be potentially positive; if and when these people can gradually come to occupy the space they withdraw into with their own presence. Then the solitude is no longer an inner one. But this is not spontaneously the case.

A dream Harry had two years after he had begun therapy well illustrates the isolation he suffered from (and also sought as a child and as an adult). In it Harry is walking through a deserted scene. The countryside around him is absolutely desolate. Along the way, he meets up with a huge peacock that is strutting along, obviously very proud of itself. This dream was very upsetting to Harry. He hated this feeling of being alone, which he had come to realize through his dreams. He knew from the dreams of his recent past that he was almost always an onlooker, a passive observer, alone and unrelated to the others. And that this was, in fact, the way he actually lived. New and quite incomprehensible for him was the huge peacock: he had no associations to it. This means that it was very far from consciousness. In fact the peacock, whose proud gait is so striking and who is so monumental, stood for his own appearance, the impression he made on others, although not wanting consciously to do so. He struggled with this idea which I, however, could only confirm, for that is exactly the posture in which he came into my office twice a week.

Harry lived a truly schizoid life, cut off from his feelings and cut off from others. The basis of this split can be seen in his truly painful childhood situation. It expressed itself in the way Harry lived with himself and with others. The split was so deep that Harry was really incapable of feeling his own emotions. In this way his case is probably most comparable with the autistic babies observed by René Spitz. Actually Harry had a similar experience to these babies: between the time his parents divorced and his mother remarried, Harry got to know many different homes, the homes of various friends of his mother. Concerned that he be well cared for while she tried to re-establish herself and get her life together after the divorce, his mother sent him away to friends. There he would stay for awhile, up to several months, until he was then sent on to other friends. And so he had been to stay with a great number of different people (whom he could no longer really remember and who seemed innumerable to him now), always getting used to the people, getting to feel at home again and again, only to be sent on after a relatively short time. It was quite understandable that separations became hard for Harry to bear. We can also fantacize that Harry, just like autistic babies, learned to turn off emotions in order to avoid the constantly repeated pains and feelings of insecurity which this life style triggered off in him.

Harry had a very long way to go in therapy. It was of vital importance for him to learn to "feel," to get a sense of himself and his emotions, to learn once again to follow up on his personal impulses. He needed to be able to establish contact with himself as an adult, and also with the child he had been. Feelings of loneliness, sadness, dejection, and self-doubt, also anger at his treatment and his solitary peacock position were all aspects of himself of which he needed to become aware. He needed to come to realize his extraordinary dependency on his present family (wife and four children), as well as on his now aged mother and her husband.

Such emotional realizations can naturally only take place when a certain degree of security has been established. A person must feel reassured that he or she will not fall apart when these so-called "weaknesses" (as they are seen from the point of view of the sufferer) have been recognized. He or she must also feel assured that the therapist will not abandon him or her when this vulnerability becomes too evident, and is even pronounced out loud.

Establishing the kind of secure situation Harry needed was extraordinarily difficult. He was very skeptical and, with his background, this was understandable. He had really not been able to learn that he could depend on others. After two years of work, the ground was more or less set: the atmosphere was such that Harry could dare open up to himself, his feelings, his long neglected inner child, and to me. We began on a long path of discovery and hence strengthening, and, ultimately, of socialization of this truly isolated individual. But doubts persisted. Anytime I was away on vacation Harry fell back into his skepticism and his accompanying fears of abandonment. All of his doubts about people surfaced once again and with a virulence. He would consult doctors, many doctors, during my absence, eager to find other reasons for his physical problems, curious about finding other, more suitable, more efficient forms of therapy. Actually, Harry was looking for security and definitely also unconsciously trying to demonstrate to himself, and to me, the abandoner, that he did not really need me as much as he did. His inner image of me as a supporting figure did not have the necessary consistency and reliability as yet. It could not easily withstand the break in contact inevitable during vacation periods. And so, during these times, for about three weeks twice a year, Harry found himself thrown back upon himself again. He was again in a room all by himself, abandoned and unloved: he withdrew from the relationship because he felt that I had withdrawn. He stood alone in his room, cut off from the outer world, and from his inner world. He lost contact with his emotional life, with his sense of disappointment, his sadness being left alone. He became identical with it and could not be with it.

With time, however, the continuity of our relationship became a reassuring fact of Harry's life. He came to discover more and more nuances of his own, personal emotional world. He dared even imagine and express other likes and dislikes than those he had allowed himself thus far. He began, for example, to think that the kind of work he was doing was not what he really wanted. It meant having to travel a great deal, having to meet customers and persuade them to buy from him. When we think of Harry's specific insecurities and, especially of his unstable self-esteem, we can realize how very demanding this work must have been for Harry. And he began to think that there might be other, better work for him. He felt that he needed to try to find a kind of job that suited him personally, although it might not please his parents. He felt the need to find a personal, creative solution, a niche in which he thought he could feel comfortable as an entire person. This was a major step in Harry's therapy, for it showed several new and important developments. Harry could feel his own dissatisfaction and define it; he could imagine doing something about it; and he could reflect on other, more suitable solutions for himself. He was well on the way to finding and coming to inhabit a room of his own. Part of his motivation for doing so was the realization of the peacock position which made him feel so terribly alone: he realized his need for feeling connected to people as the connection with himself became reestablished.

RETRIEVING THE SOLITARY SOUL

ᴥ

In conclusion to this chapter on solitude in psychotherapy, I find it most essential to underline the importance of retrieving the solitary soul from its position of retreat, from itself, and from the world. I consider this the key problem to be resolved in all psycho-therapeutic, perhaps in all therapeutic, endeavors. When a person comes to the point of feeling less alone and isolated, less abandoned and alienated from the world, then he or she spontaneously and simultaneously feels less alienated from him- or herself. This recovery from a solitary position is seminal to the healing process. And without doubt this connection—to another person, to other powers both without and within oneself—makes for the fascination which all healing techniques, religious movements, encounter groups, and seemingly scientific centers exercise upon those they have touched and brought back from the outskirts of themselves. Medical science in the past few years has also come to realize the extent to which such irrational and seemingly unscientific factors help people to get well. The recent example of post-operative patients, who healed more quickly when they were allowed to pet their domestic animals, is striking evidence to this simple, human truth. The positive healing powers of whatever was really going on in this experiment were statistically relevant. Panagoulis and his bug are not far off here.

In psychotherapy, the importance of establishing a connection is one of the tools of any serious therapist. A client who no longer feels completely alone, misunderstood, disdained, inferior, and thus unwanted and depressed, or even paranoid, is on the way to feeling at home in him- or herself and in the world. This is what happens in what is called "successful therapy." In terms of our previous images, the appropriately empathic and reliable inner image of the therapist is integrated and continues to serve the person in his or her later life. Having been allowed to get involved with him- or herself in the presence of the therapist helps the person provide the necessary space for such an encounter.

Obviously, this simultaneously means that the person can sense a connection to the various thus far rejected or split off aspects of him- or herself. The often unliked, unwanted shadow sides can be recognized as belonging to oneself. Perhaps even more essential is the sense of connection to oneself—one client called it simply "feeling connected"—that enables one to recognize the parts of oneself as parts, and no longer as representing the whole.

So often people walk around with very negative images of themselves: they are an ugly duckling or a dumbling. People can identify with negative self-images, or with negative expectations of the future, negative ideas which do not allow for development. And so we come upon those who opt for solitude, solitary souls who are too threatened by the prospect of being found.

OPTING FOR SOLITUDE

❧

Allowing another person to get close can be a threatening situation for someone not used to such intimacy. Many clients come to mind here. If all goes well, the therapeutic alliance is stable enough to allow the person to stay long enough to speak of the uncomfortableness and, perhaps, to get over it. I am reminded in this context of a young man who unfortunately could not stay long enough. He left after a few very intense sessions, during which a strong connection seemed to have been established between us. But this connection was apparently too much for him. His encapsulation is well illustrated in a painting which he did during one of our sessions (see figure 15 on page 167). In order to better explain where he was coming from, and the deeper significance of this painting, I should first explain how our work began. Merlin (a pseudonym) arrived in quite a desperate moment: depression was closing in on him. He had thus far managed to keep his feelings in check, and to run his own life well enough. But these depressive states were now just too much to handle. He would lie around feeling just horrible, very much alone and unloved, very dejected about himself and his fate. It was time to do something. During the therapy, Merlin spoke quite readily of the special role he had played in the past: the prince of the opposition, we came to call it. He became the lone hero and champion of many people, of family and friends, but also even of colleagues at work or mere acquaintances: it was always he who stood up for the poor and dejected, for the mistreated others, the victims of injustice. And he went on from one such heroic venture and relationship to the other. He, himself, had no ally, had never even confided in anyone about his own problems. He was always the one to be lending an ear to other people: he seldom even spoke about himself in an intimate way. And so, one can well imagine what a novelty the therapeutic situation was for Merlin. Here he came two times a week and talked about himself.

My first impression of this young man was that of an extremely lonely person. He spoke quite readily and within our few

Figure 15. Merlin's drawing. Used by permission.

short sessions of his style of relating, of his tyrannical father and weak mother, and of his suicide attempt at age 13. I was quite pleased that he seemed to be able to open up so well, to speak so freely of himself, and realized that this was a tremendous change for him. When he painted the picture reproduced here I still did not realize the extent to which it showed how essentially ambivalent the new situation was for him. He painted the picture in order to show how isolated he felt at home alone on weekends. Through getting involved in the feelings and trying to express them in a picture, and then in words, the situation, itself, felt much less threatening. He said his loneliness was like being alone at the bottom of the sea. From my point of view the fact that the middle spot was red and almost dead center in the picture pointed to a deep wound that Merlin seemed to feel, perhaps unconsciously, as central. He probably even identified with it: that is, this was the place where his ego was. The ambivalence of his position of isolation is revealed in the fact that the red spot is, on the one hand, definitely isolated from the rest of the ocean; on the other hand, it is encapsulated from the rest. It is almost as if he were in a specially designed undersea vessel which protects him from being invaded by the surrounding sea. It is this aspect of the situation which is the less conscious for Merlin and was also for me. It was quite apparent that Merlin had managed quite well thus far to avoid any deeper disturbances; he lived in some strangely balanced situation, was successful at work, had a circle of friends. His deeper inner loneliness had only recently begun to interfere with his feelings about himself and his life. The front, or lower part of the picture (which he said represented the waves of an agitated sea) may be related to this new agitation that Merlin was sensing, and which brought him into therapy. Essential for the failure of the brief therapy was the fact that the isolation, although it is grounds for suffering, was also part of a perfected system which functioned and which served a function. Merlin's world could stay intact if he could stay far enough away from his suffering, from his deeper feelings, and, therefore, from others. For if he really allowed anyone to get too close to him, then his suffering would become a topic which he would have to talk about. Alone, on his own, he could hold out; he could distract himself from his suffering by taking care of others.

I can only hope that sometime in the future Merlin will surface again and try to have his wound taken care of. This, itself, would bring him out of his deep isolation, but it would also threaten his self-sufficiency. The lonely hero would have to stop along the road, perhaps, and get involved in others—and in himself.

SOLITUDE AND SILENCE

As we have seen in the preceding pages, the theme of solitude has two distinct poles, the one related to darkness and dejection, the other to light and elation. In darkness fears are born: being alone is one of the conditions *sine qua non* for the birth of unfathomable fears—of horrible monsters,

intruding villains. Many are the fantastic tales of horror which ger-
minate in the silence of solitude: the phantasms of the imagination
flourish in the darkness and in solitude. These are the tales of fantasy and imagination, horrid visions of untold monsters, perhaps
like those of Saint Anthony, as we see in the paintings by
Hieronymus Bosch and Max Ernst, like the witch in Hansel and
Gretel—also a product of the venture into the solitary, dark realms
of the forest. But in light, worlds are also created, other worlds,
tales of fantasy and imagination: poems and novels, plays and
musical pieces, paintings and sculptures all are born in solitude.
Works of art are the product of solitary ruminations. Solitude and
silence brings to light that which is there: the product reflects the
spirit of its creator, be it positive and full of light and joy, or negative and full of darkness and horror. Maybe it was in this way that
God, in His solitude, created human beings—in His image, just as
man or woman in his or her solitude brings forth a creation—also
in his or her image. We can say that which lurks in the deeps, or
that which is potentially there can come to light, thanks to the
magma of solitude.

Kurtz of Joseph Conrad's *Heart of Darkness* also discovers
the potential within himself through his isolation in the depths of a
dark continent: his own shadow side. As I have said before, here in
the wilderness, outside the bounds of civilization, we can uncover
those aspects of ourselves that are not civil. Kurtz's shadow is the
epitome of what we have seen in the preceding chapters: grandiose
fantasies of his own self-worth. Kurtz discovers in himself the
grandiose tyrant, the merciless god figure who, without a second
thought, exerts his power over those around him, determining life
and death at a whim. Specific here is the fact that solitude makes it
impossible for him to get involved with these fantasies, with this
side of himself, without acting it out. He is compelled to become
that which he fantasizes. Without the grounding in his wider self,
through the appropriate inner images or ties to a society which
guarantee this identity and self-esteem, he is stranded in a sea of
grandiose visions of himself and begins to believe them. His connection to other aspects of himself and to humanity are lost.
Solitude is definitely a germinal state. Human beings need light, not

Figure 16. "Silence," Johann Heinrich Füssli (1741-1825). Zurich: Kunsthaus.

only for civilization, but also for psychic development: light stands for consciousness. Darkness stands for the unconscious, for sleep, for the dark realms of the unknown. In the dark and alone, we create our own creatures, phantoms of our own imagination. They haunt us: they create the thrill of danger. Such fantasies are always paranoid: the phantoms and monsters haunt and invade. This definitely indicates that the problem has to do with seeking other-worldly presences: we secretly hope and wish for the company of other beings, perhaps even of supernatural beings. The imagination, let loose in this free space provided by darkness and solitude, creates a universe of its own: tales of ghosts and vampires, of mysterious supernatural beings, are universal phenomena.

Psychoanalysis often involves silence, but the quality of this silence can differ immensely. When you look at Füssli's *Silence*, you see a figure bent over, closed in upon itself, with no contact with the outside world (see figure 16 on page 170). The desperation that is so well expressed in the pose well expresses the depressive tone, the hopeless dejection which can be evoked in solitude, when one feels alone and lost in an uncaring world. We have seen numerous examples of such an attitude in the preceding pages. Although this solitude is seldom consciously chosen, it is one which inevitably imposes itself when contact with the outer and inner world seems to be impossible.

In the silence of solitude one can hear one's own heart beat; this can be soothing if one feels secure within oneself, not alone; or it can be terrifying and paralyzing. Psychoanalysis knows the magic of silence, an essential ingredient in the work. But this fertile earth for any creation allows the voices within to be heard, be they monsters or surprising new inner forces. In this respect Winnicott's observations are of vital importance. The child—here the analysand—only has the possibility to contact his or her own impulses when the non-intrusive but empathic figure is there, watching, safeguarding, making him or her feel secure enough to go on into the depths of the jungle. In this respect, the analyst is like a watchful mother, a strong paternal presence, a watchman, guarding the vulnerable youth as he or she dares to go beyond the light into the dark halls of his or her own being.

ASSUMING ONE'S SOLITUDE

✌

Say in your prayers, Michel, that loneliness, desire, and longing are more than we can bear. And without them we are extinguished.[9]

As Amos Oz so well states here, the pain of solitude is quite unbearable, but we cannot exist without it. Feeling this pain is a reality of human life. Whenever we feel really close to someone, we are prone, at times of separation and loss, to feel sad and lonely. This is so and must be so, as Shota Rustaveli so well showed us over five hundred years ago. We have also seen that solitude is an integral part of the maturation process; people need to be alone, to go through periods of being alone during the normal course of their lives. Prescientific societies took such needs into consideration and instituted rites involving—one could say that they ritualized—seclusion from and reintegration into society. A moment of retreat and reflection upon oneself, of attention to the inner forces, or to the more interior voices, can help us find ever new adaptations to our changing living conditions. Phases of introversion and extroversion, solitude and sociability, are intermittent. The systolic and diastolic movements of our heartbeat, they make up the normal rhythm of human existence. Any time we tend to stay too long in either state a balance is upset.

Nevertheless, people generally tend to try to avoid the pain of solitude. We even find it difficult to speak about: most words do not seem to express poignantly enough what we are trying to say. Speaking in detail or for any length of time about our suffering from solitude just does not feel right. But all of this may just be an excuse for not getting involved with stressful emotions. The avoidance of the pain that stems from feeling alone and lonely is an important motivation of human behavior.

---

9. Amos Oz, *The Black Box*, Nicholas de Lange, trans. (New York: Harcourt Brace Jovanovich, 1988), p. 258.

Concordantly, one of the most hellish temptations we are exposed to is the pretense that we are not alone; on a large scale, trying to avoid feeling our existential solitude can be extraordinarily destructive. Many are the false "prophets of no solitude," of "you are not alone." We saw how the witch in *Hansel and Gretel* promises constancy and care, all the while actually meaning to devour the children. They cannot ever be alone—must never again suffer want—if they remain within her care, in her house, but this means that they must also remain within her power and will inevitably end up in her cooking pot: she will use them to her own evil ends. The children are not to grow up and go out into the world, but must remain in the symbiotic domain of the witch forever. In the final account, not ever being alone means the end of abandonment *and* the end of life. Where there is no separation, loss or pain there can be no development: one is paralyzed, imprisoned, devoured. Stasis is equivalent to death. Erich Neumann defined loneliness as the *principium individuationis*, in contradistinction to containment, the "basic principle of *participation mystique*, the bond in which there is no loneliness."[10]

Political movements and pseudo-religious sects often make similar promises: the "we" of posters and programs pretends the end of solitude. Their fascinating, even mesmerizing power to move masses stems from the power of the archetype of the Great Mother. If one votes for or joins the party/group, paradisical symbiotic conditions will reign: there will be an end to strife and want, to pain and abandonment. Such promises conceal a desire to hold the children in order to use them. But the need to believe in the escape from solitude is often so desperate that people succumb to temptation.

Although babies, from their first days, are constantly seeking rapport, and people focus life-long on feeling related, we are basically alone, as the final life experience so well reminds us. We are alone in our daily decisions, in our inner world. No one shares are fate. This in no way means that we are alienated from ourselves or

10. Erich Neumann, *The Great Mother: An Analysis of the Archetype*, Ralph Manheim, trans. Bollingen Series, Vol. 47 (Princeton: Princeton University Press, 1964), p. 67.

isolated from the world. Such distinctions must be made. But even when we feel at home with ourselves and in the world we realize how basically alone we are, for example, whenever we even think of expressing an opinion that is not in accord with that of the collective. Such a situation can be extremely threatening, especially when one does not feel reassured within oneself by an empathic inner figure. Assuming one's existential solitude is then inconceivable. Psychotherapy is a maturational process that can help to nurture such an inner presence. Moral courage becomes a viable prerogative of behavior in the day-to-day world and a preeminently human challenge.

BIBLIOGRAPHY

Aymès, C. A. Wertheim. *Die Bildersprache des Hieronymus Bosch.* Den Hag, 1961.

Bax, Dirk. *Hieronymus Bosch.* Rotterdam: 1979.

Beck, Aaron T. *Depression: Causes & Treatment.* Philadelphia: University of Pennsylvania Press, 1967, 1978.

Beck, Aaron T., John A. Rush, and Gary Emery. *Cognitive Therapy of Depression.* New York: Guilford Press, 1987.

The Bible: The NIV Interlinear Hebrew-English Old Testament, four volumes in one. *Genesis-Malachi.* John R. Kohlenberger III, ed. Grand Rapids, MI: Zondervan Publishing House, 1979, 1987.

Braunfels, Wolfgang, ed. *Lexikon der christlichen Ikonographie,* vol. V. Rome, Freiburg, Basle, Wien: Herder, 1974.

Buber, Martin. *Das Problem des Menschen* (1942). Heidelberg: Lambert Schneider, 1982. In English this is *Between Man & Man,* Ronald Gregor Smith, trans. New York: Macmillan, 1948.

Busch, A. *Bosch: An Annotated Bibliography.* Boston: Hall, 1983.

Chailley, Jacques. *Jérôme Bosch et ses symboles; essai de décryptage.* Brussels: Palais des Académies, 1976.

Conrad, Joseph. *Heart of Darkness.* 1902. *The Portable Conrad.* Morton Dauwen Zabel, ed. New York & London: Viking/Penguin, 1976.

Cowper, William. In Louis Untermeyer, ed. *Albatross Book of Verse.* London: Collins, 1933, 1960.

Fallaci, Oriana. *A Man.* Milan: Rizzoli, 1979; English translation, William Weaver. New York: Simon & Schuster, 1980.

Flaubert, Gustave. *La Tentation de Saint Antoine.* Translated by Kitty Mrosovsky as *The Temptation of St. Anthony.* London & New York: Viking/Penguin, 1983.

Freud, Sigmund. *The Interpretation of Dreams.* A. A. Brill, trans. New York: Modern Library/Random House, 1978.

Fromm, Erich. *Escape from Freedom*. New York: Holt, Rinehart and Winston, 1941; Avon, 1976. Published in England as *Fear of Freedom* by Routledge in 1991.

Gide, André. *The Counterfeiters*. New York: Vintage/Random House, 1973.

Gryphius, Andreas. In Volker Meid, ed. *Gedichte und Interpretationen, Band I: Renaissance und Barock*. Stuttgart: Philipp Reclam jun. n.d.

Haushofer, Marlen. *Die Wand: Roman*. Munich: DTV, 1968, 1991.

Homer. *The Iliad*. Robert Fagles, trans. London: Penguin, 1990.

International Journal of Psychoanalysis, 1958.

Jacoby, Mario. *Individuation & Narcissism: The Psychology of Self in Jung and Kohut*. London: Routledge, 1990.

———. *Longing for Paradise: Psychological Perspectives in an Archetype*. Myron Gubitz, trans. Boston: Sigo, 1985.

———. *Scham-Angst und Selbstwertgefühl: ihre Bedeutung in der Psychotherapie*. Olten: Walter Verlag, 1991.

———. *Sehnsucht nach dem Paradies*. Olten: Walter Verlag, 1980.

Jung, C. G. *The Archetypes and the Collective Unconscious*. The Collected Works, vol. 9.I. Bollingen Series XX, R. F. C. Hull, trans. Princeton: Princeton University Press, 1959.

———. *Aion*. The Collected Works, vol. 9.II. Bollingen Series XX. R.F.C. Hull, trans. Princeton: Princeton University Press, 1959.

Kafka, Franz. *Letter to His Father*. New York: Schocken, 1987.

Kiley, Dan. *Living Together, Feeling Alone*. New York: Prentice Hall, 1989.

Koestler, Arthur. *Darkness at Noon*. New York: Bantam, 1984.

Lamartine, Alphonse de. "L'isolement," in *Poetic Meditations*. William North, trans. London: H. G. Clark, 1848.

Möhrman, Renate. *Der vereinsamte Mensch: Studien zum Wandel des Einsamkeitsmotivs im Roman von Raabe bis Musil*. Bonn: Bouvier, Herbert Grundmann, 1976.

Musil, Robert. *Briefe 1901-1942*. Adolf Frisé, ed. Reinbek & Hamburg: Rowohlt, 1957, 1981.

Neruda, Pablo. *Selected Poems*. Nathaniel Tarn, ed. London: Jonathan Cape, 1966.

Neumann, Erich. *The Child*. Boston: Shambhala, 1990.

———. *The Great Mother: An Analysis of the Archetype*. Ralph Manheim, trans. Bollingen Series Vol. 47. Princeton: Princeton University Press, 1964.

———. *The Origins and History of Consciousness*. R. F. Hull, trans. Bollingen Series Vol. 42. Princeton: Princeton University Press, 1954.

Nietzsche, Friedrich. *Thus Spake Zarathustra*. Thomas Common, trans. New York: Random, 1982; or Walter Kaufmann, trans. New York & London: Penguin, 1978.

Nigg, Walter. *Grosse Heilige* (1946). Reprinted Zurich: Diogenes, 1990.

Oz, Amos. *The Black Box*. Nicholas de Lange, trans. New York: Random, 1989.

Panofsky, Erwin, Raymond Klibansky, and Fritz Saxl. *Saturn und Melancolie*. Frankfurt am Main: Suhrkamp, 1990.

Peplau, Letitia Anne and Daniel Perlman. *Loneliness: A Sourcebook of Current Theory, Research and Therapy*. New York: A Wiley Interscience Publication, John Wiley & Sons, 1982.

Petrarca, Francesco. *Dichtungen, Briefe und Schriften*. Hans W. Eppelsheimer, ed. Frankfurt am Main: Insel Verlag, 1980.

———. *The Life of Solitude*. Jacob Zertlin, trans. Westport, CT: Hyperion Conn, 1985 (reprint of 1924 edition).

Plato. *The Symposium*. Walter Hamilton, trans. New York: Viking/Penguin, 1952.

Riemann, Fritz. *Die schizoide Gesellschaft*. Munich: Christian Kaiser, 1975.

———. *Grundformen der Angst*. Munich: Masselle, 1975.

———. *Grundformen helfender Partnerschaft*. Munich: Pfeiffer, 1974.

———. *Lebenshilfe Astrologie*. Munich: Pfeiffer, 1976.

Rousseau, Jean-Jacques. *Les Confessions,* in *Oevres complètes*. préface de Jean Fabre. Paris: Editions du Seuil, 1967.

———. *Les Confessions de Jean-Jacques Rousseau*. John M. Cohen, trans. London & New York: Viking/Penguin, 1953.

———. *Du Contract Social* or *Social Contract*. Maurice W. Cranston, trans. New York: Viking/Penguin, 1968.

———. *La Nouvelle Héloïse*, or the *New Eloise*. University Park, PA: Pennsylvania State University Press, 1987.

Rustaveli, Shota. *The Lord of the Panther Skin*. R. H. Stevenson, trans. Albany: University of New York Press, 1977.

Sandars, N. K. *The Epic of Gilgamesh*. London: Penguin, 1960.

Scheller, Wolf. *Judische allgemeine Zeitung*. No. 47 (April, 1992).

Snyder, James. *Bosch in Perspective*. Englewood Cliffs, NJ: Prentice Hall, 1973.

———. *Hieronymus Bosch*. New York: Excalibur, 1977.

Spitz, René A. *Genetic Field Theory & Ego Formation*. Madison, CT: International University Press, 1962.

———. *No & Yes: On the Genesis of Human Communication*. Madison, CT: International University Press, 1966.

Spitz, René A. and W. Godfrey Cobliner. *First Year of Life: A Psychoanalytic Study of Normal & Deviant Development of Object Relations*. Madison, CT: International University Press, 1966.

Storr, Anthony. *Solitude: A Return to the Self*. New York: Ballantine, 1989.

Thoreau, Henry. *The Portable Thoreau*. Edited and with an introduction by Carl Bode. London: Penguin, 1977.

Walter, Rudolf, ed. *Von der Kraft der sieben Einsamkeiten*. Basle, Vienna, Freiburg: Herder, 1984.

Wieland-Burston, Joanne. *Chaos & Order in the World of the Psyche*. London: Routledge, 1992.

Willeford, William. *The Fool and His Sceptre: A Study in Clowns and Jesters and their Audience*. Evanston, IL: Northwestern University Press, 1969, 1986.

Winnicott, Donald W. "The Capacity of Being Alone," 39, 1958, pp. 416-420 (lecture from 24.7.57, British Psychoanalytical Society).

Woolf, Virginia. *A Room of One's Own* (1929). London & New York: Granada, 1981.

Zimmermann, Johann G. *Ueber die Einsamkeit*, 4 vols. Liepzig: Weidmann, 1784-1785.

INDEX

*J*oanne Wieland-Burston is an American analyst in private practice in Munich and Zurich. She had a Ph.D in comparative literature from Vanderbilt University, a Master of Arts in French literature from Vanderbilt, a B.A. from the University of Toronto, is a training analyst of the C. G. Jung Institute, Zurich (1990), and holds a diploma as Analytical Psychologist from the C. G. Jung Institute (1981). Her first book, *Chaos and Order in the World of the Psyche* (Routledge, 1992) has been translated into German, Swedish, and Italian editions. *Contemporary Solitude* was first published in German (*Einsamkeit*) by Kreuz Verlag in 1995 and a Dutch edition of this book will be published soon. She has lectured throughout Europe since the early 1980s at institutions including The World Council for Psychotherapy, The Deutsche Gessellschaft für Analytische Psychologie, and the C. G. Jung Institute in Munich. She continues to teach Jungian Psychology at the Jung Institute in Zurich and at psychoanalytic institutes in Munich. She lives in Munich with her family and is writing another book.